KT-165-842

From Richard
Macau – Easter
Monday 2000 ∴
(in the rain!)

Beijing ● Tianjin ●
Nanjing ◉
Liampo ● Zhoushan ●
Guangzhou ●
Macau ● Hong Kong ●
Nagasaki ●
Manila ●
Moluccas
Macassar
Solor      Timor

IMAGES OF ASIA

MACAU

*Series Editors, China Titles:*
NIGEL CAMERON, SYLVIA FRASER-LU

# Macau

CESAR GUILLEN-NUÑEZ

HONG KONG
OXFORD UNIVERSITY PRESS
OXFORD  NEW YORK

Oxford University Press

Oxford New York
Athens Auckland Bangkok Bogota
Buenos Aires Calcutta Cape Town Chennai Dar es Salaam
Delhi Florence Hong Kong Istanbul Karachi
Kuala Lumpur Madrid Melbourne
Mexico City Mumbai Nairobi Paris São Paulo
Singapore Taipei Tokyo Toronto Warsaw

and associated companies in
Berlin Ibadan

Oxford is a registered trade mark of Oxford University Press

First published 1984
Second impression 1992
Third impression 1998

Published in the United States
by Oxford University Press, New York

ISBN 0 19 583842 4

Printed in Hong Kong
Published by Oxford University Press
18/F Warwick House, Taikoo Place, 979 King's Road, Quarry Bay, Hong Kong

*This book is dedicated to the memory of Mrs A. Peñaloza de Nuñez, my grandmother.*

# Preface

THE history of Macau provides a splendid account of the way in which Western civilization, having attained a peak after the emergence of the merchant class, found itself embodied in a handful of Portuguese merchant–navigators who were seeking new markets. Irresistibly drawn towards the fabled land of the Chins, they were to find themselves cast as players in a great drama of human destiny. Their search for new outlets for trade was a search for riches and as such an act of the intellect and the will. Wealth had to be found and it had to be generated through the agency of commerce. The merchants thus sought to create new markets by bypassing the Islamic Middle East, breaking the Republic of Venice's monopoly on the spice trade, and directly establishing points of contact in the Far East.

Despite the confidence of their age these pioneer navigators were groping blindly in the dark. It is hard today to imagine those terrors of the medieval world which were inherited by Renaissance man. In his conception of the world there was great spirituality but also great fear: fear of the uncharted planet earth, of its oceans and, above all, of the phantoms of the mind. Beyond Europe and Arabia there lay exotic lands whose customs and peoples had become known to the West only through a handful of travellers' tales of dubious authenticity. Navigating by detailed charts, a few Portuguese mariners and some priests ventured with their caravels into these unknown seas. The Macau peninsula was to be their final destination in China.

The society which they created in Macau was that of a Portuguese merchant community leading its own life thousands of miles away from the metropolis. In spite of a natural Chinese cultural influence and racial absorption, a distinctive Portuguese presence permeated almost every aspect of the city's affairs; and if it is true that villains tend to dominate certain pages of the community's history it is equally true that in the end, as in a Shakespeare play, noble *senhores* appear to bring justice, restore peace and make possible the flowering of Western sciences and humanism.

The following chapters outline the historical forces that led to the founding of Macau and describe the development of the city and its art up until the early twentieth century. Constraints of space have meant that the narrative is limited to those events that best illustrate the particular characteristics of Macau's past. Similarly, the recent history of the city and its future prospects have been omitted, for they are subjects too complex to be treated in a few pages. As the book is concerned with the city of Macau, the islands of Dom João, Montanha, Heung Shan, Lappa and Malaochow, once claimed by the Portuguese as part of their territory, are not discussed. Those readers who are interested in a more detailed account of Macau are referred to the Selected Bibliography at the end of this book.

# Contents

# Acknowledgements

It would not be possible to thank everyone concerned with the making of this book. I would, however, like to acknowledge the following: Father Manuel Teixeira, Benjamim Videira Pires, SJ, and Professor Charles Boxer for reading parts of the manuscript and offering invaluable advice; the Library of the Historical Archives of Macau, and the Library of the University of Hong Kong; the photographic department of the Victoria and Albert Museum, London, and the photographic section of the Luis de Camões Museum, Macau; Henrique Nestor Rios dos Santos, SJ; and last, but not least, Mrs Gail Pirkis and Mr Christopher Homfray of Oxford University Press, Hong Kong.

# The Prayers of St. Francis Xavier

THE city of Macau, like the city of Rome, was originally built on hills: the Mong-Ha, the Montanha Russa, the Dona Maria, the Guia, São Paolo, São Geronimo, Patane (Camões) and Penha. To these there could be added Ilha Verde (Green Island) which is now merely a hill linked to the city by reclaimed land.

These hills were originally active volcanoes (as late as the 1830s earthquakes were reported) which gradually filled in the surrounding waters until the solid ground merged to form a tiny peninsula some five square kilometres in area. A narrow isthmus, one kilometre long, provides a natural bridge to link the peninsula to the island of Heung Shan in the Pearl River delta.

The mountains of the hinterland and the surrounding islands combine to act as a barrier to the wind and a breakwater, configurating a geography which was destined to provide a haven for those who arrived at its shores.

In the dynastic history of the Ming, Macau already bears its modern Chinese name of Ou-Mun, or Portal of the Bay. The Nam T'oi (Penha Hill) and the Pak T'oi (Guia Hill) at the two extreme corners of what is today the Praia Grande were thought of as the pillars of a threshold.

In days of old the traveller would walk into Macau from Heung Shan, the Fragrant Mountain, over the narrow isthmus which has often been compared to the stem of a lotus. Ahead of him there lay the hilly area known as Lin-Fa Shan and the peninsula beyond spreading out like a lotus flower, adrift on the mingling waters of river and sea. The muddy stream to left and right could, on certain days, be as still as a mirror.

Those coming in from the open sea, mostly fishermen from Fujian who were sailing down the South China Sea, knew they were entering waters sacred to the Goddess Ma, the merciful goddess of the sea, known to the Cantonese as Tin-Hau. Tradition claimed that the sea goddess had guided a ship to safety, and that she had been sighted on the shores of Macau. This led the Fujianese fisherfolk to erect a shrine on the actual spot where the miracle took place. A village existed there before the arrival of the Portuguese and soon after this, under the Ming Emperor Wan-Li (1573–1621), a temple was dedicated to A-Ma.

Portuguese galleons were first sighted off the China coast over four and a half centuries ago. They came from Malacca and initially traded offshore in the open sea. But these Portuguese merchant-navigators arriving in China were not venturing out entirely into the unknown. The China coast and the route thither had previously been charted in a collection of European and Oriental maps (some datable to 1502) in the manner of a cosmic jigsaw puzzle whose parts are gradually fitted together. The first repository for these charts, where cartographers and navigators puzzled over what were then almost insurmountable navigational problems, was probably the naval centre of Prince Henry the Navigator which is presumed to have been at Sagres. These studies were a product of the Renaissance when rational thought had begun to enlighten the educated European mind. Cartographers, astronomers and mathematicians, some of them Arab navigators, had all contributed.

Vigorous maritime expansion by Portugal reached its apogee during the first half of the sixteenth century. Two sea routes were established: these were eventually to open up the Atlantic Ocean to commerce and create new trading patterns. One of these trade routes led down the west coast of Africa, round the Cape of Good Hope, up into the Indian Ocean and thus on to

China and Japan. The other branched off from Africa across the Atlantic to the coast of Brazil. Sailors, merchants and adventurers together built a unique commercial empire that was established at a time when Portugal itself numbered no more than a few million inhabitants.

In July 1497 three ships, the *São Gabriel*, the *São Rafael* and the *Bérrio*, were sent by King Manuel of Portugal as a commercial and political embassy to the sovereign of Calicut in India. These three ships, well protected by cannon, were commanded by the brothers Paolo and Vasco da Gama. Vasco would return to Portugal a year later, with a cargo of cinnamon, pepper, ginger and other spices. His brother and over half of the original crew of 148 were to die, most of them victims of scurvy. The dreaded Cape of Storms, first reached by Bartolomeu Dias in 1488 and renamed Cape of Good Hope, had finally been rounded and the mission to India accomplished. Two years later, fearing annihilation by Islamic satellite kingdoms in the Indian Ocean, a fleet headed by Pedro Álvares Cabral avoided that region and was sent instead to Malabar. On the way they made the first official exploration of the coast of Brazil which was soon to be colonized by Portugal.

During the first two decades of the sixteenth century fear of Islamic attacks led to a more aggressive colonial policy in the Indian Ocean by the Portuguese Crown. Affonso de Albuquerque, who had put to rout the Islamic fleet at Diu, and who seized Goa and Malacca (in 1510 and 1511 respectively), would be the perfect instrument for the implementation of this policy.

Portugal was anxious to break Venice's iron grip on the Far Eastern spice trade, and to acquire a share in the Chinese market. Already in 1508, Diogo Lopes de Sequeira, surveying Malacca, carried royal instructions to enquire into the possibilities of commerce with China. After favourable trade contacts,

Portuguese merchants began to explore the South China Sea. The first known European to arrive by this sea route to China was Jorge Álvares, who in 1513 landed at a place said by the Portuguese to be called Tamão and today held to be Tuen Mun, in the territory of Hong Kong. Álvares was followed by Rafael Perestrello (a relative of Christopher Columbus) who was in turn followed by Fernão Peres de Andrade and then the ill-starred embassy of 1517 to Guangzhou and Beijing of Tomé Pires. With the failure of the Pires embassy, due in large measure to the ill will created by Andrade's brother, Simão, and to Islamic intrigues at the Imperial Court in Beijing, the first Portuguese contacts with China seemed to have come to an end. China was officially closed to them.

Not easily discouraged, the Iberians shortly found new avenues of trade in the Far East. In South-east Asia their ships reached the island of Timor and the Moluccas. Of more importance to the founding of Macau, however, was the accidental discovery of Japan in 1542 by some Portuguese deserters. Japanese traders had already been encountered in Malacca and elsewhere in the southern seas and the Europeans would certainly have known of the dreaded pirates from the Ryukyu Islands who were the scourge of the coastal waters throughout this period.

The Japan trade was now to be the impetus behind the demand for an entrepôt in China. The activities of the Japanese pirates had led the Chinese Emperor to forbid direct trading between the two countries. Ever adaptable to the volatile commercial and political conditions of the East, the Portuguese merchants soon realized the potential of the Japanese market. They were able to offer to the aristocracy goods from Europe and India and, more importantly, the silks of China which were much prized by the upper classes of Japan: in exchange they carried away silver and gold bullion.

The voyage to Japan was long and, in the typhoon season, fraught with peril. The imperative to find a secure base on the China coast where merchandise could be procured became more pressing as the value of the Japan trade grew with every year. Between 1522 and 1547 the Portuguese succeeded in establishing a handful of small trading posts in Zhejiang, Fujian and Guangdong but their histories remain obscure. Two of the first and most important were on the islands of Sheungchuen (Shangchuan) off Guangdong and Liampo off Zhejiang. Still searching, they eventually found their way through the labyrinth of South China islands and entered a district known as the Sap-Chi-Mun, facing the Macau peninsula. In about 1554 an island in this area called Lampacau became the site for an annual fair at which the Portuguese were able to purchase the silks which were so important an element of their Japan trade.

The year of the first settlement of Macau itself is uncertain but is usually given as 1557. Decades of Chinese hostility to a permanent European presence on their coast had led them to imprison many Portuguese. By 1555 some sixty of the latter were being held to ransom with high sums of money being demanded for their release. This confrontation was brought to an end by an agreement between Leonel de Souza, in command of a fleet of seventeen ships, and the Guangzhou Admiral. In a letter of 15 January 1556, written from Cochin, de Souza reported to his sponsor, the Infante Dom Luiz, that he had negotiated with the Admiral to trade in Guangzhou and to pay dues. He wrote: 'In this manner I made peace ... many Portuguese went to the city of Guangzhou and other places where ... [they] carry on their business as they please without being troubled'.

One of those other places was to be Macau. Early chroniclers refer to it as Amacau, instead of Ou-Mun. The first time that the place is mentioned is in a letter of Fernão Mendes Pinto, dated

20 November 1555, where the author says 'today I arrived in Amaquoa having come from Lampacau, the port where we were before'. Ma-Ngao is, in fact, a shortened version of Ma-Kan-Ngao, Fujianese for port or bay of Ma. From this is derived today's name of Macau, or Macao.

The diplomacy of de Souza had obtained for the Portuguese the freedom to build temporary shelters in Macau and to trade in Guangzhou—so long as they paid both customs dues in Guangzhou and a sum for the lease of Macau. Macanese tradition maintains that it was a series of naval battles against pirates, endemic to the region, that won for the Portuguese the right to settle in Macau in perpetuity. One such great battle took place in 1556 with 500 Portuguese taking part, but more fully documented in the sources available to us today is that of 1564. A Ming slab recording the grant of permanent residence is said to have been placed in the Senate; if it ever existed, it has long since vanished.

To many of the Portuguese, however, the dispensation to settle in Macau was the result neither of diplomacy nor of victory at sea. They believed that the prayers of St. Francis Xavier, a Jesuit from the Kingdom of Navarre, had been instrumental in securing the agreement. Father Valignano, SJ, commented in 1601:

the Portuguese took it that this licence had been obtained through the prayers of Father Francis Xavier himself, it being of such great benefit not only for the Portuguese but also for Christianity in Japan and China. It was not long afterwards that the Portuguese settled in the Chinese port of Amacao, which in time grew to such proportions that a fine Portuguese city emerged, such as we see now. The subsequent commerce with Japan was always carried out from there.

Francis Xavier, today considered the St. Paul of the Far East, was one of the first members of the Jesuits, and once a favourite of St. Ignatius Loyola, the founder of the Order. Sent as legate

View of the Praia Grande showing the foreign legations along the Praia; São Francisco Fort is just visible on the far right and an American steamer is to be seen in the left foreground.

Oil on canvas

44 cm × 75 cm

School of Macau or Guangzhou, *c.* 1870

Museu Luis de Camões

*The 1597 Martyrdom of Christians in Nagasaki*, detail
Oil on canvas
By an unknown Franciscan artist, seventeenth century
178 cm × 260 cm
São José Seminary

Detail of *The 1597 Martyrdom of Christians in Nagasaki* showing the martyrdom of the twelve-year-old St. Luiz; also martyred were Mexican St. Felipe de Jesus and St. Francis of Galicia.

*Pietà*
Oil on canvas
School of Macau, seventeenth century
72 cm × 54 cm
From a Santa Casa da Misericordia banner
São José Seminary

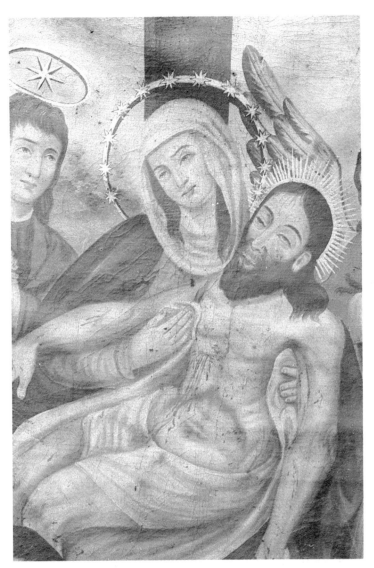

Detail of the *Pietà*

*St. Michael the Archangel*, detail
Polychrome wood sculpture, metal scales
School of Macau (?), probably seventeenth century
Height (without base) *c.* 87 cm
São José Seminary

*St. Lazarus*
Polychrome wood sculpture
School of Macau (?), probably seventeenth century
Height (without base) 115 cm
São José Seminary

*Crucified Christ*, detail
Ivory sculpture
School of Macau or Guangzhou, seventeenth century
Chapel of São Miguel Cemetery

to Goa, he had made thousands of converts in India and the Spice Islands and had boldly denounced the evils and injustices committed by local inhabitants and colonial administrators. In 1547, in Malacca, he heard first accounts of Japan from his merchant friend Jorge Álvares (who should not be confused with the first navigator who reached China) and Álvares' Japanese companion. The earliest surviving accounts of Japan by Europeans date from 1545 and are by Portuguese or Spaniards, although Fernão Mendes Pinto is often wrongly singled out as the first navigator to Japan. Xavier had grown so interested in these reports that in April 1549 he set off with a small group on his historic mission to Japan. They landed in Kagoshima four months later. However, always yearning to bring the Gospels to China, in 1552 the saint sailed down the south coast and briefly sojourned on the island of Sheungchuen some 80 kilometres south-west of Macau, awaiting favourable developments. (Videira Pires' recent studies suggest that he also halted at Hucham on Lantao Island in Hong Kong.) Xavier caught a fever on the island, and after battling for his life through the night of 2 December, died the next day. Knowing of his great love for China, to those who had finally been able to settle in Macau only a miracle seemed sufficient explanation for all that had been achieved.

## 2

# Trade with Japan and Union with Spain

THE fine city of Macau which emerged in the years following Xavier's death was concentrated in the lower half of the peninsula, between the Praia Grande and the Inner Harbour. At the end of the sixteenth century it contained about 900 Portuguese accompanied by a vast number of retainers and slaves. To the settlers' amazement, their outpost began to swarm with Chinese hawkers, peasants, coolies, sailors, merchants and craftsmen—this in spite of the fact that most Chinese were prohibited from residing in the town by their own authorities. The majority would provide essential services, and they also controlled the supply of cereals and other foodstuffs without which the traders could have survived only with great difficulty. Many of the local Chinese had skills in inland and sea navigation in the area, and would bring some of the most sophisticated craftsmanship in the world to serve the settlement and help its growth. And the comprador, an important figure in the history of Western trade with China, now also entered the scene.

Mistrustful of Macau's growth, the Chinese built a wall in 1573 across the isthmus to the north which gives access to Heung Shan—like the Great Wall it was intended as a barrier against the encroachments of barbarians. This smaller wall, to become known in Portuguese as the Porta do Cerco, created an effective stranglehold at the neck of the peninsula, at first only opening twice a month to allow the flow of goods to Macau. Said to have been built to prevent thieving in Heung Shan by black Portuguese slaves, from quite early on it became primarily a tool for political manipulation by the mandarins.

Despite these hindrances the Portuguese were not now entirely excluded from the Empire, and from the year 1575 the traders were permitted to sail twice a year to the city of Guangzhou. Tribute in the form of large sums of money and gifts had to be offered to the Viceroy or, in his absence, to the Governor of Guangzhou on landing and on departure from the city for the right to buy merchandise there. This merchandise consisted mainly of raw white silk. It was carried in bulk in special barges to Macau where transactions began for bale space in the convoys to Japan, Goa, the Spice Islands and elsewhere. Large revenues were received from the 3 per cent Portuguese tax known as the *caldeirão*: derived from the profits of the Japan trade, these revenues were put towards the upkeep of the city.

The unregulated beginnings of Macau had made of it a kind of plutocracy, ruled and administered through juntas of the wealthiest merchants in control of the trade. But once it fell within the larger sphere of the Portuguese Empire, it soon became subject to the Indian territory of Goa and part of the domain of the Captain-Major of the Japan Voyage. To all intents and purposes this latter office carried with it the privilege of the Governorship of Macau for as long as the particular Japan voyage lasted—normally about a year. The appointment lay with the Portuguese Crown and bestowed on the appointee the monopoly of the trade for that year. (Portuguese trading elsewhere in the world was organized on a similar basis at this time.) Sometimes the appointee might sell his right to the office and it later became the practice for the appointment to be auctioned in Goa.

The Captain-Major would be the supreme authority in the city as long as he was physically in it—usually during the long monsoon season. Amongst a long list of Captain-Majors several names stand out, namely those of Leonel de Souza; Tristão Vaz da Veiga, extremely important as first Captain-Major of the port of Nagasaki; Lopo Sarmento de Carvalho; and André Pessoa, gallant captain of the *Nossa Senhora da Graça*, who in 1610, his ship being embargoed by Japanese officials in Nagasaki, fought off 1,000 Japanese and withstood the enemy's attacks for three nights until, outnumbered by an armada in Fukuoka, he finally had his ship blown up with himself in it. There was also an attempt to appoint a permanent captain for Macau and we know that Diogo Pereira occupied this position from 1562 to 1564. A letter written by João Baptista do Monte, SJ, informs us of this appointment and of the fact that Pereira had been a 'great friend of St. Francis Xavier'.

These early years also saw the creation of the post of *Ouvidor*, or Chief Justice, and of a Bishop, with the Bishopric of Macau being created in 1576 to include China and Japan, an indication of the city's growing importance. Less than a decade earlier, a Jesuit from Lisbon, Melchior Nunes Carneiro, had stopped in Macau. He was Bishop of Nicea, created such by Pope Julius III, and had been confessor to St. Ignatius Loyola. Melchior Carneiro did not waste any time: he proceeded to found hospitals for Portuguese and Chinese, a leprosarium and other charitable institutions—including the Santa Casa da Misericordia 'to provide for all the poor', as he states in a letter. The city's first Bishop, Leonardo de Sá, Bishop of China, would arrive two years before Dom Melchior Carneiro's death in 1583 to find the groundwork laid for him by this saintly man.

A few years before Bishop Carneiro's death news reached Macau that Dom Sebastião, King of Portugal, had fallen at the battle of Alcacer Quibir on 4 August 1578.

Although the sixteenth century was Portugal's Golden Age, from the 1540s on a succession crisis threw the nation into confusion, for no less than eight of King João III's heirs had died.

Prince João, his last remaining offspring, died before the birth of his only son and heir, Dom Sebastião.

During Sebastião's childhood his grandmother, Catherine of Austria, acted as Regent. She favoured an alliance with Spain, but Cardinal Henrique, his aged great-uncle, backed by the Jesuits, sought a patriotic solution to the crisis by insisting on a purely Portuguese line. However, the Cardinal's plans were dashed by the disastrous course of action pursued by his great-nephew.

As King, Dom Sebastião proved idealistic but irresponsible. Even at the age of twenty-four, his only reaction to Portugal's dilemma was a determined effort to escape reality: he roamed the Kingdom with his court, settling nowhere, like a medieval knight in search of a cause. Moors were by now openly harassing Portugal's coastal towns on the Algarve and Sebastião became obsessed with a private scheme to defeat the infidel. Brushing aside the advice of councillors and the nation—and even a portent in the form of a large comet which had flown over Portuguese skies—at the end of June 1578 he set off for Morocco with a badly organized army of 24,000 made up of Portuguese soldiers and Italian, Spanish and German mercenaries. At the plain of Alcacer Quibir the enemy, outnumbering and brilliantly outmanoeuvring the Portuguese army, massacred most of them. Amidst the carnage lay the body of Dom Sebastião.

At home, after the initial shock and grief there soon arose a bitter political and legal conflict for succession. There were two main Portuguese contenders, Catherine of Braganza and the Prior of Crato (an illegitimate son of one of Dom João's brothers); but there is little doubt that the rightful heir was Philip II of Spain. In June 1580, Philip arrived at the Spanish-Portuguese frontier in Badajoz to review his troops and prepare for an entry into Lisbon. He had come to claim and take by force if necessary the Portuguese throne he had inherited through his mother, Isabel of Portugal.

Philip's claim was supported by many of Portugal's nobility. However, he was not popular with the people. In order to prevent the accession of the popular pretender, Dom António, Prior of Crato, Philip crossed the frontier and occupied Portugal. The following year his claim was accepted in the historic Courts of Tomar, on the condition that the King swore to keep the Portuguese and Spanish Crowns legally and politically separate. The same applied to the administration and commerce of the two nations' colonies. The first world empire in history had been born.

To anyone researching the subject, it seems absurd that Macau should have kept up the kind of defiant attitude to the Dual Monarchy that is attributed to it in the popular imagination. However, feelings of humiliation and defeat were real enough in Macau as in the rest of the Lusitanian world. In fact, final acceptance of the Habsburg Emperors was only achieved in Macau in 1582 through the mediation of Bishop Carneiro and others, and through the able diplomacy of the Jesuit, Alonso Sanchez.

For sixty years three Philips of Spain were to rule over Macau. Royal decrees, missives, senior appointments and political moves were to be ratified or made directly by these sovereigns. The fifteenth-century Papal edict of *Mare Clausum* whereby most of the world's oceans were closed to any but Iberians was now a reality. Portuguese soldiers would triumph and fall for the Habsburgs and in the great historic tide that had overtaken Portugal Macau was inexorably caught.

The union of the Crowns was not entirely detrimental to Portugal and its trading empire. The colossal scale of colonization in Brazil, for example, became possible only after it. Macau itself, in the opinion of the modern Portuguese historian, Joaquim Serrão, gained a greater importance as an entrepôt, given the proximity of the Spanish Empire in the Pacific. The trade with Manila and indirectly with the New World was so profitable that the Tomar prohibitions, whereby Philip of Spain had vowed to keep separate the Spanish and Portuguese Crowns, were largely ignored. At one time the trade route between Macau, Manila and Acapulco became the most lucrative of its kind in the world. Constitutionally Macau would at this time develop and mature. The city now became aware of itself, and more permanent structures appeared—in spite of Chinese decrees. It also developed a form of administrative body which reminds us of the more democratically advanced city-states of Europe. This was its Senate House. The historian, Andrew Ljungstedt, later came across a manuscript which stated that 'by permission of Dom Duarte de Moneyes, Viceroy of Portuguese India, the assembling took place in April 1585 ... the plurality voted for a municipality: they proceeded to mould it by selecting from among themselves two judges, three aldermen, and one procurator'.

Macau was now important and large enough to claim for itself the rank of city. This was officially granted by Philip II on 10 April 1586, with privileges equal to those of Evora in Portugal. The King further decreed the confirmation of its name as *Cidade de Nome de Deus*.

As Macau's opulence and renown grew, due mainly to the Japan trade, a number of Jesuit missionaries on their way to China or Japan sojourned in it: men like Matteo Ricci, and later the influential João Rodriguez Tçuzzu, Adam Schall and others, who brought the deeper values of European civilization to the Far East. Invariably housed in the Jesuit College popularly known as São Paolo, their contribution to what became a famous centre of learning has never been properly studied. It was in fact as a young man in this College that Ricci, a mathematician and astronomer, learned to speak Chinese.

At the Jesuit College in Rome and at Coimbra University in Portugal, Ricci had distinguished himself as a young scientist. He was sent to Goa in 1578, and later, now ordained a priest, to Macau for the China mission. He had first entered southern China as the companion of a fellow Italian Jesuit, Miguel Ruggieri. Both missionaries were following in the footsteps of some fifty priests from Portugal, Spain, Italy and even Mexico, who from the 1550s had sojourned in Fujian and Guangzhou; this at a time when China was officially closed to the outside world.

Insisting on respect for the civilizations and traditions of Eastern peoples, Ricci began his mission with a deep investigation of Chinese culture. Only after twenty years of patient study and missionary work were the doors of the capital city suddenly to be opened to him. He arrived in Beijing in 1601 accompanied by Diogo de Pantoja; summoned to audience with Emperor Wan-Li, they presented gifts from their Macau College. Delighted by the novelty of two chiming clocks, the Emperor decided to allow a Christian mission in the capital. Ricci was already conversant with the Chinese classics and could hold intellectual discussions with members of the scholar class. This led to his friendship with the scholars Xu Guangji and Li Zhizao, both his students, from which emerged the famous translation into Chinese of the *Elements of Geometry* and the *Guide to Mathematics*. Equally important was Ricci's introduction of Chinese culture to the West. Such was his fame that contemporary records in the *Ming Shi* state that Ricci was known and respected throughout the Empire. Soon after his death in 1610, there were 150,000 Christians in China.

Obviously the innovative scientific thought in the fields of

mathematics, geometry, astronomy, geography and other subjects, which Ricci had introduced to the Chinese Court in
Beijing, must have formed a part of the curriculum at the Jesuit
College in Macau. As a complement to the College, in 1588 the
Jesuits introduced to the city a printing press with movable
type, a radical improvement on the original Chinese invention
of woodblock printing. This new kind of printing, which
would make the dissemination of the written word universal,
was greatly admired by the Chinese. But greater still was their
admiration for the Portuguese science of artillery and the novel
firearms being cast in the city.

# 3

# The Spirit of So Few

THE guns at Monte Fort, today for ever pointed at some invisible enemy, remind us that by the turn of the century war—often in the form of sudden raids from the sea—had become prevalent in the Iberian world, and was as much a part of life as the plague or the Inquisition. They also remind us that firearms, formidable bronze cannon, had ensured Portuguese sovereignty in their overseas dominions. Although today no bell, trumpet or distant drummer is heard in Macau's old forts, on the morning of 24 June 1622 the city came alive with the roar of cannon-fire. Dutch warships, the *Gallias*, the *Groeningen* and the *Engelsche Beer*, had attacked São Francisco Fort which was badly exposed at the northern end of the Praia Grande.

As a diversion the enemy had started a well-planned offensive the afternoon before, on the eve of St. John the Baptist's day. On 24 June, however, it had renewed its artillery fire with a ferocity that warned the city's Captain-Major, Lopo Sarmento de Carvalho, that the expected invasion of Macau was imminent.

The attack was not a novel occurrence. It was one in a series of sea raids that the Dutch and English had kept up for decades on Iberian shipping and coastal towns in Europe, America and the Far East. The Dutch had been particularly active as regards Portuguese possessions. By 1630 Pernambuco and north-eastern Brazil would be taken. In the Far East, in 1605, under Admiral Maatelieff, they had occupied most of their rivals' possessions in the Moluccas and the following year had practically annihilated the Portuguese fleet off Malacca.

An extremely complex political situation brought the Dutch

into conflict with Spain. Although the ostensible reason was the Thirty Years War which was then devastating Europe, events were to show that the real aim of the Dutch was the capture of the fabled riches which, like a river of silver, streamed from the New World and the Far East into Lisbon and Seville. The capture of Macau, Malacca and Nagasaki would mean tapping the river at one of its main sources.

Coen, Governor of Batavia and a staunch Calvinist, had visions of ousting the Spaniards and Portuguese from their strongholds in the Far East with a view to establishing by force a Dutch trading empire in their place. A first objective was the subjection of Macau which would then serve as a strategic base for attacks on Malacca and Manila.

The operation was to have been a joint Anglo–Dutch one, but the two English ships taking part pulled out after a last-minute disagreement concerning the invasion and looting of the city.

Coen, it appears, was extremely well-informed about the state of Macau's fortifications for the following was contained in the intelligence report sent to the invading fleet: 'Macau was always an open place without a garrison, which ... could easily be taken by a force of a thousand or fifteen hundred men'.

The Dutch were to send 13 ships under Commander Cornelis Reijersen, with some 1,300 men, including Japanese and other mercenaries, on board. The report further noted:

they [the Macanese] brought twelve cannon from Manila, whence another five guns are expected. They would gladly fortify the city but the Chinese would not allow it ... at the present time there are some 700 or 800 Portuguese and Eurasians in Macau besides about 10,000 Chinese.

The invaders were to find only the Portuguese and Eurasians, together with their black slaves. The Chinese had all fled. This exodus highlighted the Portuguese predicament: the Captain-Major reminded the Macanese that if they should let themselves be defeated, they could expect no refuge in China. The fight was to the death and the very nature of the struggle filled the citizens with a spirit of heroism.

On the morning of the engagement, the *Gallias* was so badly damaged by artillery fire from São Francisco Fort that it was put out of action. The bulk of the Dutch fleet, headed by the 400-ton *Zirckzee*, captained by Reijersen, prepared for the real invasion. Between 600 and 800 troops readied for a surprise landing on the north-west side of the peninsula, on Casilhas beach. Under a barrage of gunfire the Dutch force landed and fought its way up Casilhas, even after Admiral Reijersen was badly wounded by a stray bullet. This part of the territory is dominated by Guia Fort. It is also the highest point of the peninsula. It was along Guia Hill, towards the city, that the invaders advanced.

Captain Ruffijn took over command of the force but as his men and cannon came within shooting range of Monte Fort a thundering explosion shook his ranks. By firing two cannon shots from Monte Fort, which was manned by the Jesuits, Father Rho had blown up a barrel of the invaders' gunpowder. In disarray, the Dutch tried to reach Guia Hill but came under fire from a small contingent of men stationed there. At this point their resolve faltered and they retreated, whereupon Carvalho, aided by Captain João Soares Vivas who had arrived from São Tiago Fort, harangued the populace in the name of the Virgin and St. James with such fury that they fell on the enemy in a rage.

The rest has passed into legend. Captain Ruffijn was killed. The Dutch fled in panic to their boats, as emboldened Bantu slaves, many of whom had been drinking heavily, set about severing the heads of their stricken enemies. Of their own dead, excepting slaves, the Macanese counted only 4 Portuguese and 2 Spaniards, against some 300 of the enemy.

In the ensuing euphoria many black slaves became free men, and the Guangzhou Admiral sent them 400 piculs of rice as a tribute to their loyalty and valour. The victory had brought everyone, Oriental, African and European, momentarily together. As an eighteenth-century chronicler was to put it: 'Those Portuguese, and a few Spaniards who were here, worked wonders that day ... for although it is true the enemy did not put up the resistance it could have, one cannot help but admire the resolute spirit of so few against so many'.

The nomination of Macau's first Captain-General, or Governor, came as a direct result of these attacks by the Dutch. The Senate had petitioned the Viceroy in Goa for a proper garrison for the city commanded by a captain who—unlike the annually appointed Captain-Major whose sole motivation was the safety of the Japan fleet he commanded—would be there to defend the city at all times.

The Senate was to get more than it bargained for. A new post was created for a Macau Captain-Major with mainly military duties and powers. The first such appointee, Francisco Mascarenhas, was nominated in Goa in May 1623 with a salary of 300 *cruzados*. He arrived in Macau in July of that year to a very cool reception. The powers granted to him aroused the resentment of the local plutocracy. So badly did things begin that Mascarenhas found it necessary to retreat to the Monastery of Santo Agostinho, just behind the Senate. His detractors proceeded to fire three shots from São Paolo Fort: these passed through the Monastery walls, but nobody was injured.

According to a contemporary, the Italian Marco d'Arvalo, Mascarenhas collected the cannon-balls and had them gilded, after which 'he sent one to the King, the second to the Viceroy, and kept the third for himself'.

Mascarenhas' reaction was fairly characteristic of future un-welcomed Governors. After biding his time, he eventually tricked his way into Monte Fort with a small garrison, occupied it and converted it into his official residence, whilst expelling the Jesuits who owned it. From now on, if anyone aimed guns from here it would be the Governor.

Having established his position, Mascarenhas' first priority was the strengthening of the city's defences. His subsequent completion of São Paolo Fort, and the building of São Francisco and São Tiago Forts to defend those points where the city's waterways were most vulnerable, show him to have been a Governor protective of his community as well as of its interests as a centre of commerce.

In keeping with these policies, he ordered a wall to be built running from São Paolo Fort down to Patane in the Inner Harbour. But there was a local political peculiarity with which Mascarenhas and his successors were not entirely familiar, namely the susceptibilities of Ming officials. Corruption had become chronic in the Ming Court after the death of the Wan-Li Emperor, and only the Senate understood the workings of Chinese politics. Understandably alarmed at the sight of the wall, the Guangdong mandarins ordered its destruction. Partial tearing down of it in March 1625, together with a judicious distribution of bribes, was sufficient to set their minds at ease. Mascarenhas finally accepted defeat in order to avoid the blood-shed which might have followed from a confrontation.

Contrary to popular belief Mascarenhas completed his three-year term of office—the normal duration of the Governorship—quite successfully. However, certain political events did mar his record, the most injurious of which was the construction of the Patane wall already referred to, an incident in which his brash-ness had merely exposed the limitations of his office.

From the resistance which the first Governor encountered it

can be inferred that in the city, from then on, the figure of the Governor was to be identified with the authorities in Lisbon and Goa. The Senate, in particular, was to assume a defensive stance and quickly consolidated its role and rights as sole representative of the people, at least to the south of the Porta do Cerco. For it must be remembered that at this time the Senate, the *Câmara*, was a large meeting-hall where, in theory, those citizens who were included in the limited political franchise of the time could gather and vote. Although in practice the Senate came increasingly to be dominated by the wealthiest members of the community, at this time its democratic ideals could be realized due to the small number of eligible citizens.

The end of the third decade of the seventeenth century was the end of an era for Macau. Philip IV of Spain, pathetically attempting to retain a wasted empire—whose ruin was largely the result not only of his predecessors' mistakes but also of the corruption of his own administrators—could no longer counter the English and Dutch offensive.

The Dutch were the more intent on conquering Portuguese dominions in the Far East. The clash of 1610 between André Pessoa, captain of the *Nossa Senhora da Graça*, and the Japanese had been partly due to the fact that the Dutch had gained a foothold at Hirado in Japan. Portuguese misgivings over this development were to be confirmed. A ruthless competition developed, with Dutch ships waylaying Portuguese convoys all the way from Goa to Nagasaki. Dutch intrigues fanned the flames of the hatred expressed by the Japanese Shōguns towards Christian converts. Charges of sedition were trumped up against them and Iberian missionaries: many of those lucky enough to escape the persecutions and gruesome tortures which beset them from the beginning of the seventeenth century, found a haven in Macau. The situation reached a deadlock when indebted Macanese merchants failed to satisfy Japanese financiers. By 1636 the

Portuguese had been relegated to an inferior trading port at Deshima by the Japanese authorities, and even this was finally closed to them in 1639. The following year only 13 out of an embassy of 74 Portuguese, Macau Chinese and Africans sent to Japan by Macau were spared; the rest were executed. The fabled Japan trade had come to an end.

In 1641 Dutch harassment of Portuguese commerce culminated in the capture of Malacca which had served as port of call between Macau and Goa. A ten-year truce was signed by the two nations in the following year: it was, however, largely disregarded by the directors of the Dutch East and West Indies Companies who were determined to expand Dutch influence in the Far East. The cold war with Protestant Holland continued for the rest of the seventeenth century, with the Jesuits in Beijing thwarting Dutch initiatives to establish diplomatic relations with China. The Dutch, as we have seen, had paid the Portuguese in the same coin in Japan, and were achieving a political and cultural splendour that would make them a world power.

The reaction in Portugal to Habsburg losses of Portuguese possessions provoked the party of Braganza loyalists to wrest power from Philip IV in 1640. News of the restoration of the House of Braganza was delivered in Macau on 30 May 1642 by António Fialho Ferreira, sent directly from Lisbon by King João IV with instructions for the Senate. The citizens' delight on hearing of the restoration bore witness to their deep loyalty to Portugal. By Ferreira's account, the city had been rent by strife and dissension engendered by the despotism of its Governor, the obese and brutal Sebastião Lobo da Silveira; at news of the restoration, however, 'the enmities were ended with everyone making up amidst embraces and tears'. Feelings of solidarity would be short-lived, and Braganza rule did not bring the benefits expected, either in Portugal itself or in its overseas

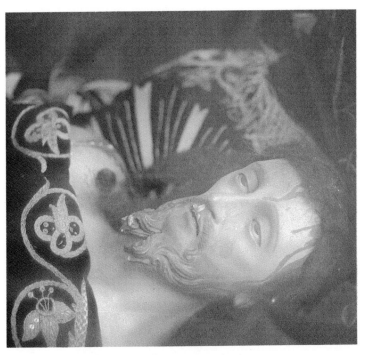

*Recumbent Corpse of Christ*, detail
Polychrome plaster with velvet and gold cloth
Probably Portuguese
São Domingos Church

*Life of St. Francis: St. Francis Denouncing His Father*, detail
Oil on canvas
School of Macau, seventeenth century
248 cm × 214 cm (with frame)
From São Francisco Church, now in São José Seminary

*Life of Francis: St. Francis talking to the Birds*
248 cm x 214 cm (with frame)

*Life of St. Francis: The Ecstasy of St. Francis*
248 cm × 214 cm (with frame)

Solomonic columns in the Tabernacle of Our Lady, detail
Silver columns, with mother-of-pearl in the entablature above
Macanese, dated 1683

São Paolo Fort
Mainly seventeenth-
century

Belfry of São Paolo Fort

A Macau villa, detail
Early twentieth century

A Chinese house in
Macau, detail showing
Chinese windows and a
European balustrade
Early twentieth century

*Portrait of a Chinese Scholar*
Oil on canvas
School of Guangzhou,
*c.* 1860
Museu Luis de Camões

possessions. But in Macau the acclamation and celebrations that marked the restoration are a golden page in the history of the city.

In 1644 Lobo da Silveira ended his inglorious Governorship of seven years by training the cannon of Monte Fort upon the people for three days—until a procession of the Blessed Sacrament made him come to his senses. His successor, Carvalho de Sousa, had him imprisoned in São Tiago Fort for his excesses.

As if parallel destinies dictated great historical changes, in 1644 the Ming dynasty fell to Manchu invaders from the north. The Portuguese had supported the Ming and had instructed Chinese soldiers in the use of cannon in Beijing in 1629. Now great waves of refugees fleeing the Manchu hordes poured into Macau, so that at one point the steps of São Paolo were daily strewn with the sick and the starving. The Manchu victory meant that from now on Macau would have to deal with Manchu officials. In 1684 one of the most corrupt of these, the *Hoppo*, or Customs Superintendent, established an office at the far end of the Inner Harbour.

Portuguese influence in the Far East was further reduced when the profitable Manila trade, which had been brought to a halt after the restoration of 1642, was again prohibited by Governor João de Sousa Pereira in September 1654—after a foolhardy attempt by Manila Spaniards to lure Macau back to Spain. Macau's economic situation was serious indeed, for in addition, with the disappearance of the Japan trade, and the severing of the sources of silver at Nagasaki, its traders no longer attended the Guangzhou fairs. However, the merchants found new markets in Indo-China, Macassar (where the Manila trade continued indirectly and illegally up to 1668) and Timor and, although a war was to develop amongst rebel Timorese towards the end of the century, the city survived and prospered.

Continued loyalty to Portugal was given recognition when King João ordered a heraldic inscription to be placed before the Senate's entrance, where it is still to be seen. It bears the words: 'City of Nome de Deus, there is none more loyal'. Then the following explanation is added: 'In the name of the King, our Sovereign Dom João IV, the Captain-General of this fortified town, João de Sousa Pereira, ordered this notice to be displayed as a witness to the great loyalty of its people'.

# 4
# Power Struggles, Civil and Religious

From the end of the seventeenth century Macau found itself now on the periphery and now at the centre of a whirlpool of politics and religion. In 1693 there had been revived an old and violent disagreement between the various religious orders who sent proselytizing missions to the Far East over the attitude to be adopted towards ancestor worship and the state cult of Confucius—the central components of Chinese family religion and imperial ritual respectively. By the beginning of the eighteenth century, Macau's religious establishment had polarized into two rival camps. One was headed by the Jesuits who held—as they do today—that these traditions were not idolatrous: indeed it was under Jesuit influence that Pope Clement IX had approved the incorporation of these cults into the practice of Catholicism in China. The other was led mainly by their constant rivals, the Dominicans and the Franciscans, who held the opposite view.

The disagreement, which became known as the Rites Controversy, now revived with fresh vigour and reached such proportions that by the start of the eighteenth century it had involved both Pope Clement XI, who had decided to dispatch an envoy to the East to investigate the problem, and Emperor Kang-Xi, who was deeply baffled by the intricacies of dogma. Like the Ming Emperors, whom his court emulated in an attempt to rid itself of the stigma of its barbarian past, he kept a number of Jesuit savants as advisers, men who would bridge serious gaps in Chinese knowledge of mathematics, geography, medicine, artillery, astronomy and musical theory. Practically all of these men, including Tomás Pereira, a Portuguese priest who had already prevented a war between China and Russia with the signing of the Treaty of Nerchinsk, often interceded on behalf of Macau and of Christianity. Meanwhile, in Rome, the Jesuits were attempting to persuade the Pope of the need to accept the practice of Chinese customary traditions.

Clement XI now hand-picked a competent but inexperienced young prelate, Charles Thomas Maillard de Tournon, to travel to the East to look into the question of the rites, and bestowed on him the title of Patriarch of Antioch. Tournon disembarked in Macau in April 1705, *en route* to Beijing. Almost from the start, his sense of self-importance must have made him unbearable to the elderly Bishop of Macau, João do Casal.

Annoyed at the tensions which developed in the city, the young prelate left for Beijing where, in ill health, he was first granted audience by the Emperor in December of the same year. Kang-Xi received him with all the honours due to his rank—at one point offering him a drink from his gold cup—and took rather a fancy to him. For a moment it looked as if another fruitful relationship like that between Adam Schall and Emperor Shun-Zhi, Kang-Xi's father, who had made the old Jesuit a mandarin of the first rank, might develop. With the astronomer Jacome Rho, SJ (who had fired the famous shot from Monte Fort in 1622), Schall had reformed the Chinese calendar. He had also introduced Western optical and hydraulic instruments to the Imperial Court. Shun-Zhi was greatly attached to him and made him tutor to his son who was later to become the Emperor Kang-Xi.

However, neither Tournon nor Kang-Xi could withstand the force of events. Nor could they reject the roles that fate had chosen for them. China's high degree of organization made of the Empire a vast beehive of which the Emperor was the nucleus: his semi-divine status was expressed through the meticulous ritual of the Court. But Kang-Xi revealed himself to

Tournon as a practical middle-aged man who was the loving father of 26 children. The Emperor was a Confucian scholar and a shrewd administrator: his ready appreciation of new ideas from the West contrasted sharply with the narrow-minded intolerance of Tournon.

Kang-Xi gradually lost patience with the intruder and his persistence in condemning rites that were hallowed by tradition. Tournon constantly ignored the advice of the Jesuits at Court who argued that the rites did not go against the spirit of Christianity. He was finally ordered to leave Beijing ten months after his arrival. Undaunted, he proceeded to Nanjing where he issued his famous prohibition, instructing all missionaries to reject the rites *sub poena excommunicationis*.

Now the Emperor finally ordered Tournon back to Macau and arrested his secretary. Following his arrival in the city the heat of the old controversies revived in reaction to Tournon's condemnations and his quarrels with Bishop Casal. Casal flatly refused to publish the Nanjing decree. Indeed he ordered all ecclesiastical authorities to ignore it. Moreover, Goa had sent word to the city that the Pope and his legate were contravening the *padroado*, the Portuguese prerogative regarding the China missions. Lisbon had never granted a permit for Tournon to proceed to Beijing.

Informed of this turn of events, the Viceroy of Goa (not the Emperor Kang-Xi, as is sometimes argued) ordered the confinement of Tournon. He was held custody in comfortable quarters in Santo Agostinho Monastery and received visitors, pending deportation.

The Pope rewarded his legate by making him a cardinal in August 1707. Tournon learnt of this while still in residence in Macau. He would eventually die in the city in June 1710 and would be buried in the cathedral whence his remains were later transported to France.

Religious troubles in Macau resulting from his Nanjing edict had started before his death. In September 1709 Tournon's partisans, the Prior, Pedro do Amaral, and his fellow friars from São Domingos, were put in prison, and only set free thanks to the intervention of Bishop Casal. After Tournon's death the friars of Santo Agostinho, again at the instance of the Goa Viceroy, were deported to Goa for similar reasons. They would not be able to return to their home in Macau until a decade later. In spite of the conciliatory efforts of a later legate named Mezzabarba, the Rites were finally condemned by the Roman Inquisition of 1710 and then by Pope Clement XI in 1715. Missionaries were now compelled to take an oath to strive to abolish them. Not until 1940 did the Papacy retract its condemnation.

The year of Tournon's death was an infamous one. It was in mid-February of that year that the Senate had clashed with Governor Diogo de Pinho Teixeira who was unconstitutionally claiming civil powers. In an unprecedented move, the Senate had left the Senate building and set up the *Câmara* in São Paolo College with the Jesuits as mediators. In answer to this, the Governor had ordered the election of a new *Câmara* and the result was two administrations.

In order to force the rival Senate out, Teixeira aimed the Monte cannon at the College. Meetings at the beginning of June to solve the stalemate had little effect and the discontent led to open combat in the streets between the citizens and the Governor's supporters. This conflict provoked the Senators into coming out of hiding to hold a meeting in the old Senate House. Aiming to stop this, on 29 June 1710 Teixeira and his guard made their way to the Senate, but found the path barred by a mob. After a skirmish which resulted in several deaths, Teixeira returned to Monte Fort and, in emulation of an earlier Governor, Lobo da Silveira, had the guns trained on the people swarming before the Senate. One of three shots flew in through the Senate door knocking dead a porter and wounding several people as it crashed on the granite steps inside.

Bishop Casal intervened at this juncture in a characteristic way, by having the Blessed Sacrament taken to Monte Fort in solemn procession while the city's bells began a plaintive toll. The psychological manoeuvre was a success. Governor Teixeira called off the attack and came out of the Fort to kneel before the Sacrament. The dispute ended the next day and reason had triumphed, but only thanks to the intervention of the Church. The Senate resumed its regular seat after the arrival of a new Governor a month later.

The citizens and their representative, the Senate, had vindicated their rights; Casal continued to serve his city by founding the first ecclesiastical chapter the following year. In 1735 he and the Bishop of Beijing (the incumbent of a bishopric that dated to 1690) became joint Governors of Macau—some twenty years and ten governors after the notorious religious and civic disturbances that had so marred the first decades of the century. By then this enlightened man was ninety-five years old and his wise leadership lasted only a few months before his death.

# 5
# Ambassadors and Merchants

THE controversies of the first decades of the eighteenth century were but a manifestation of more ominous undercurrents which beset Macau like a mysterious plague. Travellers of the period were to reflect on the passing of the city's prosperity in the wake of the decline in its trade. In a perverse way, the impoverishment of the city acted as a foil to the glitter of historic embassies and to the fashionable supercargoes of the British East India Company who began sojourning in Macau in elegant mansions, veritable antechambers to their Guangzhou factories.

The spectre of poverty was often the result of maladministration and of impossible political relationships with Goa and China. But there were also serious errors in Macau's efforts to expand trade. Alexander Hamilton, writing in 1727 as an eye-witness in his *New Account of the East Indies*, reported that if Macau 'in the Forepart of the seventeenth century ... was the greatest Port of Trade in India and China ... [that] rich flourishing City has ruined itself by a long War made with Timore ... They have exhausted their Men and Money on that unsuccessful Project of domination ... out of forty Sail of trading Vessel, they have not above five left'.

Hamilton was exaggerating: there were other equally important factors that contributed to Macau's ruin. But he was generally correct in his perception. From 1664 to 1730, Macau, the leading partner in the lucrative sandalwood trade with Timor, became entangled in the endless internal revolts of the Timorese by sending aid to the unpopular governors appointed from Goa. The Macau that Hamilton saw early in the eighteenth century was still architecturally beautiful but, nonetheless, deeply impoverished. By mid-century the Portuguese had virtually given up the sandalwood trade in Timor, together with that in slaves, horses and honey.

Fortunately, the city was now to benefit from an unexpected bonanza. Emperor Kang-Xi, acting on a 1717 memorial from an official serving in Guangdong who decried the invasion of China by European commercial and religious interests, issued a number of edicts to check the foreigners. One of these prohibited Chinese subjects from trading with any country save Japan.

This protectionist measure severely disrupted the profitable Batavia tea trade, re-routing it via Macau. The year 1607 had seen the first Dutch shipment of tea from Macau to Java and some three years later Java received its first cargo of tea from Japan. The Dutch also transported the first shipment to Europe and later, via Batavia, to New Amsterdam in America. From then on, the demand for tea in Europe and America developed with an extraordinary momentum. The demand was inflated by the interest shown in the beverage by the European nobility. Thus Princess Catherine of Braganza of Portugal, on marrying Charles II of England in 1662, had introduced tea to elegant society in England. From this new fashion there were large profits to be made. At the time of Kang-Xi's imperial edicts, tea was already supplanting silk as the main item of export in the China trade, and in Holland it was becoming the most lucrative. By the 1760s Dutch and English ships alone were carrying ten million pounds of tea per annum. For four glorious years, as a result of capturing the Batavia market Macau's volume of trade increased considerably: in one year alone the number of ships registered jumped from 9 to 23. Unfortunately, in 1720 the lure of high profits led the Chinese authorities to create the *Co-Hong* monopoly of merchants at Guangzhou to deal with foreign trade.

Equally damaging to the city was the Senate's rejection in 1719 of the proposal of Emperor Kang-Xi that the European factories at Guangzhou be transferred to Macau. This refusal elicited strong protests from Dom Luis de Meneses, the enlightened Viceroy of India, for it would, in fact, have turned Macau into one of the wealthiest ports in the Far East. By the time his opinion prevailed, Kang-Xi had died and Yong-Zheng, an Emperor not at all partial to Europeans, had ascended the Imperial throne. Even then, the same offer made to Macau after a lapse of thirteen years was again rejected.

The dissipation of commercial gains was due in part to infighting or maladministration in government circles, but also to outside meddling by Chinese mandarins, and to natural disasters. Already in 1709 the *Ouvidor* had put the *Procurador* under arrest for three days. The post of *Ouvidor*, or Chief Justice, was itself to be abolished temporarily in 1740 following complaints that its authority had been abused. As for natural disasters, the *Black Boy* and *Corsario*, 2 of the 11 ships reported to have been lost to the city between 1735 and 1745, foundered in the fearful typhoon of 1738. Believed by contemporaries to have been the worst typhoon since the founding of the colony, it swept the sea up as far as São Domingos Church. Coinciding with Macau's nadir was the consolidation of China's cultural and political power. The Manchu Empire now extended over some four and a half million square miles, while the area of Macau peninsula occupied by the city did not go much beyond two square miles. By mid-century, as opposed to China's 150 million souls, Macau's Christian population counted no more than 5,000 of whom the vast majority were non-European women. It was at this time that Macau was referred to as 'the city of women'. A large number of these were child slaves (abandoned or sold by poor Chinese parents) or prostitutes. Many of the abandoned infants were reared by the Santa Casa da Misericordia, but only up to the age of seven. After that, they had to fend for themselves.

Macau's difficulties were compounded by the dependence of the Macanese community on China for provisions. Chinese merchants dominated the retail trade and the hawking of agricultural goods was carried out by local peasants. The disproportionate number of Chinese inhabitants was a constant source of anxiety to the Portuguese. A special meeting of the Senate had to be called on 21 May 1713, to discuss 'the great harm which has been caused to the city ... due to the multitude [of Chinese] who live scattered over many houses, villas and shops'.

Manchu hegemony had the direct result of strengthening Chinese authority within the city. The most aggressive of China's new policies was the creation in 1744 of a *Tso-Tang*, or Macau mandarin, with administrative powers over the territory, almost a provocation to Macanese claims to self-rule. Then in 1779 there appeared on the Praia Grande a second *Hoppo*, or Customs Superintendent, complementing the Inner Harbour *Hoppo*. However, it is a measure of the city's adaptability that these political changes only enhanced its Sino–Portuguese character. Now both Chinese and Portuguese sovereigns were joyously feasted on accession to the throne and mourned at death. Unfortunately, serious administrative dilemmas were inevitable.

Political, judicial, commercial and religious authorities in Macau were soon at loggerheads with Chinese officialdom. Several perfectly straightforward cases became excuses for a show of strength. The best known of these, occurring in 1744, involved a homicide committed somewhere along the steep lane called Travessa do Tronco Velho, just to the right of the Leal Senado, when a drunk Chinese by the name of Chan Fai-ch'in collided with a Macanese known as Anselmo. In a scene worthy of the Spanish painter Goya, a quarrel ensued, and Anselmo drew a knife and stabbed his opponent several times. Such violence had been fairly typical in Macau since the middle of the seventeenth century or before—erupting mainly between Macanese or even Japanese sailors.

The Portuguese authorities now came into dispute with the Magistrate of Heung Shan, the Chinese administrative district in which Macau lay. It appears the Macanese had found Anselmo guilty of manslaughter and were treating the case accordingly, whereas the Chinese Magistrate insisted on a conviction for murder. Moreover, it was demanded that the Chinese legal system be enforced. On such cases its verdict was simple: a life for a life. Anselmo was finally hung in the bazaar quarter of the city in front of Macau's *Procurador* and the victim's parents. This conclusion to the case dramatically restated the old Chinese demand that, where Chinese subjects were involved, Chinese law should take priority. The above case led to the creation of the post of *Tso-Tang* and may have provoked the Guangdong Viceregal edict of December 1749 regulating conduct between ethnic Chinese and 'Macau barbarians'. An edited version of this was placed in the Senate itself.

Another important incident involved Governor António Telles de Menezes, called *lofu*, or tiger, by Chinese residents as a result of his stand against both Portuguese and Chinese opponents. Attempting to stamp out corruption amongst local administrators, he would invite them to his residence for a drink. Half-way through the visit they would suddenly be dealt a severe beating. His intransigence reached a climax when he had the matshed wall of the *Hoppo*'s compound torn down by his negro slaves as he considered it an affront to Portuguese sovereignty. He had, doubtless quite knowingly, injured the *Hoppo*'s rank and made him lose face.

It was a dangerous test of strength. The horrified Senate had the wall re-erected at its own expense and finally forced the

Governor out of office with the aid of the machinations in Goa of Manuel Vicente Rosa—one of the wealthiest and most influential Macanese. Menezes, the Tiger, left the territory under arrest.

Concurrently with these happenings, the hornets' nest of religious extremism so inopportunely stirred by Tournon at the start of the eighteenth century now turned its fury on Macau. The banishment and persecution of Christians in China which had begun in 1723 was enforced in the city. At the intervention of the Bishop and the Jesuits this had little effect on the Macanese, but Chinese converts were constantly harassed. Those gathering at the Church of Nossa Senhora do Amparo, situated at the end of the stepped Calçada do Amparo just below São Paolo, were ruthlessly punished. By the end of the century, vengeful imperial magistrates had all but stifled Christianity in China proper and had rigorously suppressed the religion amongst the less well-protected converts of Macau.

The despotism of the mandarins had a counterpart in Portugal in the reign of terror imposed by King José's favourite minister, Sebastião de Carvalho e Melo, later Marquis of Pombal. The long arm of his private vendetta against the Jesuits reached Macau on 5 July 1762 when at 3 o'clock in the morning the Jesuits were arrested and herded into ships bound for Lisbon. Treated like slaves and transported in the hold, several died on the way, a spectacle calculated to please the Minister.

For Macau the effects were disastrous. In the words of Charles Boxer in his book, *Fidalgos in the Far East*, 'The expulsion of the Jesuits also dealt a severe blow to the economic condition of the colony. Foreign observers were unanimous in their opinion that the commercial decline of the city was greatly accelerated by the loss of its most energetic and competent administrators'.

At the same time as these civic disorders there was a parade of European embassies *en route* for Beijing. Portugal sent the splendid Menezes embassy in 1715, and that of Pacheco Sampaio in 1752. On arrival in Macau, this last ambassador was sumptuously housed in a silk pavilion.

One of the most important, if most tragic, missions was that of Lord Macartney, King George III's special envoy. On his return from Beijing in 1794, he was housed in an elegant mansion just outside the city walls. Known at the time as the Casa Garden, it was the property of a wealthy English East India merchant.

Lord Macartney's mission, like that of several envoys from England before him, was not a success. In a chilling rebuff, Emperor Qian-Long decreed:

Your Ambassador requests facilities for the ships of your nation to call at Ningbo, Zhoushan, Tianjin and other places for purposes of trade. Until now trade with European nations has always been conducted at Macau, where the foreign hongs are established ... For the future, as in the past, I decree that your request is refused and that the trade shall be limited to Macau.

As for George III's request for 'remission or reduction of duties on merchandise discharged by your British barbarian merchants at Macau', this was also refused. For, as the Emperor had noted, 'my capital is the hub and centre about which all quarters of the globe revolve'.

Behind the apparent vanity of Qian-Long's statement there lay the disturbing truth that China was then the largest empire on earth. Macau was a mere speck of dust in that vast strange universe that revolved about the Emperor, a pebble on the sea-shore that could be washed away without trace by an unfavourable tide of history.

# 6

# The Yearning for Liberty

IN the latter half of the eighteenth century, the Senate had locked horns with successive governors in a desperate bid to retain its autonomy. Attempts by the Portuguese Crown to bring the Senate into step finally came under Queen Maria I, at the instigation of the Colonial Minister, Martinho de Melo e Castro. In April 1783 the *Providências da Corte* (Court Regulations) came into effect and the Senate was made subordinate to the Governor's authority: the latter now increasingly infringed on the Senate's traditional privileges.

A telling passage of the Regulations reads:

The Governor has been excluded from all the decisions and dispositions of the Senate, without any exception, even where they concerned the good or evil administration of the Royal Treasury ... The Senators of the *Câmara* of this important dominion, composed in the majority of exiles who there took refuge ... ignorant of all manner of government and with no other aim but to procure their personal gain through navigation and commerce, are only concerned with making less cruel the tyranny of the mandarins with servile self-abasement and distribution of bribes ... with no concern whatsoever for the decorum of the Portuguese nation.

In an attempt to boost the Governor's powers the office of *Ouvidor* or Head Judge was revived. Its powers also encroached on those of the Senate, so that the office was one of the most influential. The first such *Ouvidor* was Silva Ferreira, to be followed in 1797 by Pereira dos Santos and in 1802 by Miguel de Arriaga Brum da Silveira. Arriaga was to become a powerful opponent of those who sought a more liberal constitution in the city.

By the beginning of the nineteenth century the nature of political theory and practice in Europe had been ineradicably transformed by the events and example of the French Revolution. King João VI had returned to his throne in Portugal, after the years of exile in Brazil during the Napoleonic Wars, to face serious opposition to a reimposition of absolute monarchy. A settlement was finally achieved by a new constitution drafted to effect a transfer of power from the Sovereign to the people.

This state of affairs in the mother country found an echo in Macau and a local Liberal Party was formed. Early in 1822 a petition to King João was drafted by Miranda e Lima, a prominent Liberal. This sought a restitution of the Senate's old privileges and Lima also demanded a suspension of subsidies to Goa and Timor, and that all senior civil and military posts in the city should be reserved for local Macanese.

Governor José Ozorio de Castro Cabral had little sympathy for such Liberal reforms. The obstinate refusal to compromise by either side brought the confrontation to a head in the feverishly hot summer of that year. To resolve the crisis a general assembly was called on 19 August, presided over by the Governor. Popular elections were won by the Liberals, as had been expected. Led by a Major Paulino da Silva Barbosa, they now attempted to impose their authority over the city.

On 20 August Cabral was asked to resign his post. He was offered the traditional powers conferred on Governors which would confine his authority to that of a military commander. The deposed Governor, swallowing his pride, wrote in a proclamation that this 'is the greatest glory to which I could aspire', but then added in a more ominous vein: 'My future conduct will prove to you the sincerity of my feelings'. He was escorted to his residence by a cheering crowd to the strains of a military band.

A mere three weeks later, Cabral led a first revolt, but his later *coup d'état* on the night of 15 November had a greater impact.

The Liberal Government retaliated to the revolts with sum-
mary arrests made, it seems, in response to the demands of an
excited mob. One of the first to be detained was the *Ouvidor*,
Miguel de Arriaga, who had been dismissed from his post. Two
days after the first Cabral-led coup, a *canaille* poured through
the streets and stormed his residence, trapping him inside, while
others ran across the Leal Senado square clamouring for his
arrest. Arriaga was eventually carried off by two Senators and
the enraged crowd to Monte Fort where he was imprisoned.
Cabral and his fellow conspirators were also put under arrest.

The city was now infected with a mood of anarchy. Exiled
conservatives in Goa were busy undermining the Liberals. A
group of them, calling themselves *Os Imparciais*, complained in
an issue of the *Gazeta de Goa* that 'such is the state of disorder
and confusion that reigns in that city, that the accusations of a
mere drunkard are sufficient to stir up the entire city, and for a
meeting of the Senate to be called on the night of 2 December'.
The reason for the emergency meeting was charges that Arriaga
had tricked his way out of jail. The charges were not very far
wrong: Arriaga, who had been allowed to return to his house in
response to his plea of poor health, eventually weaseled his way
out of Macau and into Guangzhou in the middle of 1823.

The Judge's escape was to prove fatal to the Liberals, and the
crisis was compounded by the arrival in Macau waters of the
frigate *Salamandra* from Goa. This warship had been dispatched
by the Viceroy of Goa to effect the downfall of the Liberal
regime. Gathering his forces, Arriaga reminded the Guangzhou
Viceroy of past collaborations (including action against piracy).
After the latter had surreptitiously sent a man to Macau to
report back on the situation, he agreed to lend his support to the
Judge.

The part played by the *Salamandra*, with a crew of 69 men
under the command of Joaquim Garcês Palha, was dramatic

indeed. It was checkmated from June to September by Major Barbosa, who aimed the guns of São Paolo Fort at the frigate. But with the backing of the Guangzhou Viceroy and Baron São José de Porto Alegre, one of the richest merchants in Macau, Palha was able to land in a boat with a handful of men and take control of the fortresses. His main troops came ashore later.

Orders from Goa were immediately put into effect and an interim government was created, with Bishop Cachim as Acting Governor. Major Barbosa was arrested and deported to Goa along with several prominent Liberals. Others, such as the Editor of the *Abelha da China* (originally the Revolution's mouthpiece), fled to Guangzhou. Miguel de Arriaga returned and Captain Palha would later be named Governor.

In an uncanny duplication of the history of the revolution in Portugal, Macau's glorious Liberal Revolution had been unceremoniously snuffed out less than a year after it erupted. Political change would, however, materialize after the fratricidal wars which broke out in the 1830s in Portugal between the two brothers, and heirs to the Crown, Dom Pedro and Dom Miguel. With the triumph of Dom Pedro's brand of Liberalism, new constitutional reforms were enacted in Macau in February 1835, under the Governor, José de Sousa Soares de Andrea. The most important change was a curtailment of the Senate's administrative powers, by partitioning the administration between the Governor and his council on the one hand, and the Senate on the other. The Senate was reduced to a municipal *Câmara*, dealing with the administration of urban affairs and subject to the Governor.

On 20 September 1844 Macau was made a province independent of Goa but was reunited with Solor and Timor in the first of a series of constitutional reunions with the now impoverished Timorese.

# 7

# Twilight of Empires

IN the first decade of the nineteenth century Portuguese sovereignty over Macau had once again been brought into question when the British, now masters of the oceans after their brilliant defeat of Napoleon's fleet, twice entered Macau waters claiming to be coming to the aid of the city as Portugal's ally against France. In 1808 they actually disembarked and occupied the Guia and Bom Parto Forts. Governor Lemos Faria was not deceived by this fallacious argument; however, under pressure from the British Admiral, and against his better judgement, he finally allowed the British forces to land. The Chinese authorities were much opposed to such a landing—and rightly so, for six years earlier the British had already devised a plan to take Macau. In a letter of 30 October Lemos Faria informed the British Admiral, William Drury, that the Senate was parleying on Britain's behalf with the Chinese, but firmly stated that: 'As I have already told you and now repeat: of the Macanese, not a single one but gives his allegiance to the House of Braganza'.

In view of Drury's intransigent refusal to vacate the Forts and the city, Judge Miguel de Arriaga sought the assistance of Chinese officials. Faced with a hostile Imperial edict and a superior Chinese force, Admiral Drury reluctantly left Macau on 20 December. Although the Chinese Emperor was very likely merely following tradition in defending a tributary territory under China's suzerainty, Arriaga became the hero of the moment and of future Portuguese generations. In spite of the dark shadow of his trafficking in opium, his high reputation was confirmed after his masterful handling of the surrender of the notorious Chinese pirate, Kam Pau-sai, in 1810.

Some thirty years later Macau found itself once again caught in the middle of an escalating conflict between China and Britain. The financial solvency of the Indian Empire had recently become dependent upon the silver bullion with which the Chinese bought the cargoes of opium that were shipped from Calcutta. In 1839 the controversy over the opium traffic between European merchants and the Chinese government came to a head. Lin Zexu, Governor of Hunan and Hubei, who had been appointed Imperial Commissioner in charge of the elimination of the traffic, forced the foreign firms out of Guangzhou where they had previously practised this trade in spite of frequent protests by the Chinese authorities. Captain Charles Elliot came up from Macau to mediate and two months later shipped all British subjects to safety in the Portuguese territory.

Opium addiction had been a social problem in China since the early eighteenth century but, like snuff taking, it was then comparatively insignificant. In 1729 only about 200 chests of raw opium had entered China for use by addicts. A hundred years later 6,000 chests per annum were being shipped to Lintin Island and on up the Pearl River. In the year of the Guangzhou débâcle 30,000 chests entered China. Although the traffic was condemned as much by the European powers as by China, it continued nonetheless, albeit in smaller volume, and was not to leave Macau until the early twentieth century. Behind a mask of declared abhorrence for the evils of the drug, both parties continued to reap handsome profits from it, whether through trade and taxation or bribery and corruption.

The events leading to the British exodus from the colony now relentlessly followed their unhappy course. The British traders who had been expelled from Guangzhou persisted in their traffic in Macau and Commissioner Lin threatened a march on the city. Governor Silveira Pinto, fearing a massacre, asked the entire British community to leave. On 26 August 1839 a pitiful crowd of men, women and children (both the guilty and the innocent) huddled on the Praia Grande as the evacuation began. The fleet of vessels and boats which transported them eventually disappeared with its anguished exiles over the horizon, headed towards Hong Kong.

As for Macau's Chinese community, its gratitude to Lin Zexu knew no bounds. The local people rejoiced that at last somebody in China had stood firm against the hated opium traffic brought by the foreigners. Celebrations broke out throughout the city with parades and the erection of decorative structures and *pai-lou*. The Emperor's Commissioner entered the city in September 1839 at the head of a long procession in which he was directly followed by the Viceroy of Guangzhou. Lin himself was carried in an eight-bearer sedan-chair in a victory march which culminated on the Praia Grande. Offerings were made in thanksgiving to Kun-Yam, Goddess of Mercy, at her ancient temple in Mong-Ha.

The Macau government's behaviour was diplomatically impeccable. A troop of soldiers met the Commissioner, and gun salutes were fired as Lin's cavalcade passed Santo António Church near the old Protestant cemetery and the Casa Garden.

On advice from his representatives in the Far East, the British Foreign Secretary, Lord Palmerston, now determined that force must be used to persuade the Emperor of China that Her Majesty's subjects must be granted the freedom to trade. Superior firearms dictated the course of this First Opium War: the Emperor's representatives were compelled to treat for peace at the negotiating table. The Treaty of Nanjing of 1842 ceded to Britain the island of Hong Kong: once the latter had begun to develop as a trading port it attracted the troublesome British away from Macau.

The Nanjing treaty was the first of a string of Chinese treaties with European nations which now bore witness to Manchu capitulation to the West. One of the most historic, the Sino–American trade treaty, was signed by Caleb Cushing, the American Minister, and the Governor of Guangdong in Macau's Kun-Yam Temple in Mong-Ha, on 3 July 1844. This was the very temple where offerings had been made during Commissioner Lin's victory march.

New hope for a revival of the city's pride and prosperity came with the appointment as Governor in 1846 of João Ferreira do Amaral. Amaral, a naval man, came with instructions from Lisbon to reconstitute Macau as a free port and to consolidate Portugal's sovereignty.

He abolished the Portuguese customs (which had been set up in 1783), annexed the island of Taipa which lies just to the south of the main peninsula, and forced Chinese fishermen to pay taxes. To make extensions to the overcrowded city and to create the space to build three roads, the area from Monte Fort up to the Porta do Cerco was cleared of squatters, small farms and graveyards. Amaral also achieved his ultimate goal: the expulsion from Macau of both *Hoppo*, the Chinese customs officials. The Governor's authority was underlined by the solemn demolition of the pavilions of the *Hoppo* in the Rua de Nossa Senhora do Amparo.

Amaral was undoubtedly both heroic and compassionate. But the desecration of graveyards showed that he adhered rigidly to the narrow ideals of military men of his generation: several of his measures appear to us intransigent and unrealistic. Likewise, a rather absurd event was turned, by his intervention, into an international incident. This was the jailing at his orders of James Summers, an English chaplain visiting a Macau regatta, after the latter had offended traditional sentiment by refusing to remove his hat like everyone else during a Corpus Christi procession. When a British rescue mission came to set Summers free, a man was killed and the dispute ended only with the intervention of Lord Palmerston, the British Foreign Secretary.

Owing to his expulsion of the *Hoppo*, Amaral's most bitter enemies now included the authorities in Guangdong. The streets of Guangzhou were hung with posters offering a reward for his head. Seven assassins disguised as beggars came forward and, on the afternoon of 22 August 1849, he was cut down from his horse and murdered as he rode near the site of his building scheme at the Porta do Cerco. The conspirators vanished across the border with his head and left hand (he had lost his right hand many years before).

An interim Council of Government was immediately formed and it decided to occupy the Porta do Cerco with a Portuguese garrison. A mere three days after the assassination, the garrison was readied when a force of 2,000 men in the Chinese fort known to the Portuguese as Passaleong was seen to be preparing for combat. It was at this highly critical point that a Macanese lieutenant, Vicente Nicolau de Mesquita, with a contingent of only 36 men, and before the astonished eyes of local and foreign spectators, braved the one-mile run to Passaleong Fort under a barrage of fire and captured it as panic-stricken Manchu soldiers took to their heels. The Fort was later blown up. Both Amaral's death and the lieutenant's bravery spurred other European nations to a show of solidarity against Chinese aggression; the British, in particular, showed great judgement by sending a frigate.

China's domestic plight was now aggravated by a major revolt inspired by a millenarian ideology which incorporated certain elements of Christianity. The Taiping Revolution against the Manchus broke out in 1850 and was only put down by a joint Sino–European operation after much blood had been shed. For Macau this, and similar disturbances later on, meant the perennial influx of desperate refugees from the mainland.

The Porta do Cerco would from this time onwards serve as a checkpoint to hinder Chinese entry into the colony. The cultural and technological development of European nations in this era was such that many Westerners became excessively conscious of Europe's collective attainments. After the eighteenth-century craze for Chinoiserie had evaporated, the stagnant state of Far Eastern civilizations became painfully evident to all. Europeans now experienced feelings of shock, then of disdain, for the conditions they encountered in the Orient. Fortunately for Macau, the Christian discipline of compassion was now well established in the city in a variety of forms. The community was spared many of the more abhorrent and inhumane results of European intolerance. Neither Chinese nor Western writers could fail to observe the spirit of fraternity between Portuguese and Chinese which was often encountered in Macau.

In 1862 the Portuguese felt that they also should take advantage of China's weakness and press for sovereignty over the territory they occupied. In August of that year a treaty was drafted, and negotiations started in earnest in Tianjin after some skilful lobbying by Isidoro de Guimarães, one of Macau's longest-serving and most respected Governors. Negotiations continued in a mood of discord under Coelho do Amaral, and dragged on until 26 March 1887 when the thorn in the 'treaty of friendship and trade', Article II conceding sovereignty in perpetuity, was accepted, and the treaty was signed by Governor Tomas de Sousa Rosa. During the late 1850s and 1860s a number of foreign legations and embassies, all jostling for a part on the Chinese stage, had their first headquarters in China set up in Macau, often along the Praia Grande, taking advantage of the colony's improved status. Their presence lent a new prestige to the city and enhanced the quality of its society and culture.

By the middle of the nineteenth century wealthy indus-
trialists and merchants were coming in from the mainland and
bringing skills and capital with them. This new breed of en-
trepreneur Chinese was largely the product of contacts with
the West and some of them, such as the famous Howqua in
Guangzhou, were amongst the richest men in the world. New
social conditions saw a surge in traditional industries such as silk,
tea and fireworks, with the manufacture of bricks being introduced later. The introduction of new industrial concepts from
the West was the catalyst for Macau's economy to expand into
new areas: previously it had been very much limited to trade.

Such endeavours suffered a serious setback in 1874 when a
killer-typhoon, one of the worst in Guangdong's history, struck
the city. In neighbouring Hong Kong 2,000 people died and 35
ships were sunk as harbour waters lashed the Praia. In Macau,
the havoc was even worse, with losses mounting up to two
million patacas. To increase the destruction a violent fire broke
out during the typhoon (some claim that it was deliberately
started by looting arsonists). Another great typhoon would
follow in 1902.

In the interim between these two typhoons it became painfully clear that Hong Kong and the other treaty ports had begun
to eclipse Macau. One of the main reasons was the introduction
of the steamship; but, long before its regular use for cargo, the
rising costs of storage in Macau had meant that Chinese junks
and international shipping had begun to bypass its harbour
altogether. With the advent of the steamship, and then other
forms of motorized vessels, the process became irreversible. The
result was fewer trans-shipments and more direct transactions
between Chinese ports and Hong Kong.

As the buildings and harbour facilities of the British colony
multiplied inexorably, Macau found itself trailing behind, its
historic heritage crumbling into ruin, its once-famed Inner

Harbour declining into a provincial port for fishing vessels of shallower draught. By the end of the nineteenth century, the administration frankly accepted that Macau was now only an intermediary between Chinese ports and Hong Kong. The fishing industry had become its main source of income.

In a peculiar way, the importance to the territory of its fishing industry enhanced its Lusitanian character, for it now gave the impression of being a Portuguese fishing village which had somehow become inhabited by Chinese. During the first decades of the twentieth century Macau was the main fishing port of South China, in spite of pirates and exorbitant taxation by China. All the same, the unloading of cargoes of tea, silk, fans and other items, which had continued over the centuries, was becoming a thing of the past.

There were sporadic attempts to revive the old glory, and some impressive land reclamation and quaint city embellishments and housing improvements resulted. But at the same time that Coelho do Amaral had initiated his ambitious city planning, gambling, prostitution, the opium traffic and the infamous coolie racket (which came to replace child slavery, abolished by an outraged Portuguese monarch in 1759) began to supplant more lawful but now less promising means of making money.

The one project which could have saved the city from financial stagnation, the building of an artificial harbour deep enough to service international tonnage, found itself enmeshed in procrastination and uncertainties. First plans for work on the Inner Harbour were drawn up in 1884 by the engineer Adolfo Loureiro, but they were never carried out. Other harbour plans were presented during the first decade of the twentieth century, and work was finally initiated under Governor Álvaro Machado in 1911. But by then a whole new political world was about to be born.

Portugal had become a Republic in 1910. The Manchu and Russian Empires were on the brink of collapse and the First World War would soon disturb the international scene. A troubled monetary and political situation also meant the rise of illegal activities in the territory. Manuel da Silva Mendes, a Portuguese expatriate advocating social reform and forming part of a group of intellectuals which flourished at this period (it included the poet, Camilo Pessanha, and a young Chinese doctor, Sun Yat-sen, who was then residing in the city), decried the lack of a proper public library or a local museum; the undeveloped state of the government-run secondary schools; the irresponsible destruction of the city's heritage; and the corrosive effect of unchecked gambling on the citizens of Macau. However, as Mendes himself admitted, the Portuguese-language primary schools run by the Leal Senado were adequate, as were hospitals and a number of charitable institutions. In spite of the drain of talent and capital to Shanghai and Hong Kong, Macau retained a calm, and a sense of proportion, which made it one of the most agreeable and genteel cities in the Far East.

# 8

# Churches and Temples

First accounts of the city of Macau by chroniclers and travellers of the late sixteenth century tell of the great number of religious buildings (characteristically ubiquitous in an Iberian city) and discuss the state, impressive or indifferent, of the fortifications. Macau was intended to be a *praça* or fortified town, as were most Portuguese colonial towns of the period. However, in the case of Macau, political conditions allowed that stratagems for defence should come second to aesthetic considerations. Like other Portuguese settlements, Macau began simply as a cluster of dwellings gathered about a natural vista selected for its beauty and charm. Such an arrangement was quite unlike the rational grid pattern of Spanish colonial settlements. One need only think of Bombay (Bom Baía, the Good Bay) in India, or of Rio de Janeiro in Brazil, to understand the inspiration behind the Portuguese metropolis. From early on, the Praia Grande with its two citadels of Penha Hill to the south and Guia Hill to the north was the focus about which radiated the city of Macau.

On the peninsula there emerged three major districts, later to become *bairros* and parishes denominated Sé, São Lourenço, and Santo António. To these were added those of São Lázaro and, in our century, Nossa Senhora de Fatima, both originally outside the city walls. In time more popular *bairros* and squatter settlements were annexed and acquired colourful names such as Patane, Tarrafeiro, Matapao and Bazar. The rich gamut of Cantonese village life was soon being absorbed in counterpoint to the rhythm of the Portuguese metropolis.

The Jesuits were amongst the most active pioneer patrons of

the developments of the early sixteenth century. Six of Macau's most important religious, educational, social and military structures appeared thanks to their initiative. Apart from the magnificent fortress, the principal of these was undoubtedly the College and Church of Madre de Deus, or São Paolo. To Dom Melchior Carneiro, SJ, was due the city's first leprosarium with its Hermitage of Our Lady of Hope (in time to develop into the Church of São Lázaro), and the patronage of other Jesuits sponsored the building of the Church of São Lourenço, and the Sé (Cathedral), both started between 1550 and 1570. The Seminary and Church of São José, one of the city's grandest building complexes, was founded by members of the order in the early seventeenth century.

The city's nucleus was formed after the founding of the Senate in the 1580s, in the square now known as the Largo do Senado. The roughly triangular square extant today may have acquired its form in this early phase. At the base of this isosceles triangle was located the *Câmara*, or Senate. The right face of the triangle was formed by the Santa Casa da Misericordia and its Church, with its distinctive granite portal which was probably surmounted by a granite relief of Our Lady of Mercy. An equally characteristic castellated stone tower stood to the right, and in front there was the gibbet which lent a somewhat medieval aspect to the whole.

There is no record of the appearance of the left face but, bearing in mind that it must have retained something of the character of a medieval European town hall square, it may have consisted of a row of private and public buildings, as it does today. It was probably in the sixteenth century that, just behind this row, there developed a market, which led, as it does now, to the square where the São Domingos Monastery is located. Today only the general disposition of the main buildings gives an indication of the original layout: apart from the relief of Our

Lady of Mercy, now in the Leal Senado, practically nothing remains. Fragments of information from contemporary chronicles, and the detail of early nineteenth-century drawings permit only the barest of reconstructions. Judging from these drawings, the Santa Casa seems to have retained much of its seventeenth-century appearance into the last century; now, however, it is radically changed.

If the Largo do Senado was the municipality's civic centre, its spiritual and emotional heart was and remains the Jesuit Church of Madre de Deus and the ecclesiastical buildings that surround it. Today this once-famous ensemble is reduced to a gutted ruin. Only the granite façade of the Church still stands, over twenty metres in height. One reaches the platform by climbing a grand flight of seventy granite steps. Once at the top the visitor passes through the main portal of the façade and enters, not a glittering Iberian church interior, but a sterile void. This was once the great Church of São Paolo, celebrated in the 1630s by such chroniclers as Peter Mundy, Father Alexandre de Rhodes and Father Antonio Cardim. Father de Rhodes wrote:

Dans le temps auquel les Portugais y avaient le trafic libre, ils baftirent au College de noftre Compagnie une fi belle Eglife, que ie n'ay rien vue qui l'egalle, mefmes en toutes les belles Eglifes d'Italie; à la reserve de Saint Pierre. (At the time that the Portuguese had free commerce there, they built at the College of our Company such a beautiful church, that I have not seen anything that can equal it, even in all the beautiful churches of Italy, except St. Peter's.)

The account goes on to describe the fine and spacious architecture of the interior whose walls were covered in gold from ceiling to floor. Evidently the splendid façade which survives today was only a prelude to the marvels that lay within. The vault of rare Japanese wood was carved by Chinese craftsmen, but in the typically Portuguese style known as *talha*. The construction of the Church from designs by the Italian Carlo

Spinola, SJ, began in 1602. The façade, largely the work of Japanese artists, was started and finished in the 1630s. These artists and craftsmen worked under the direction of Italians, but the unknown designer of the façade created an architectural structure known as a 'retable-façade' which is characteristic of Spanish architecture. This cosmopolitan masterpiece was made possible in the tolerant, civilized milieu that prevailed in many an Iberian settlement. The interior and façade of the Church, and the College and Library, were monuments to Macau's golden age. A humble straw shelter built in December 1565 was the first of four earlier structures to be burnt down by Chinese marauders in search of plunder. On each occasion there arose out of the ashes a new building always superior to its predecessor. It is said that the last conflagration in 1835 was an accident started in the kitchen of the College when, after the dissolution of the religious orders in Macau the year before, the buildings served as a barracks for Portuguese soldiers. But the granite façade withstood the blaze and still stands majestic and peaceful, transcending the human passions which often shape the history and destiny of man.

Of the golden seventeenth century with its voyages to Japan and elsewhere precious little remains in the city. All that survives are a handful of religious images of ivory and wood; the silver tabernacle of São Domingos, with its Solomonic columns, which is dated to 1683; a number of oil paintings on canvas in which the hand of a local school of artists may be seen (one of them is a particularly beautiful pietà, once the reverse of a Santa Casa da Misericordia banner); and various later images and architectural features.

Four of Macau's most famous monasteries and convents were Spanish foundations and three of these date from the period of Habsburg rule between 1580 and 1640: Santo Agostinho (1586), São Domingos (1588), and Santa Clara (1633). The priests and nuns who founded them came from the Philippines: impressed by their faith and devotion the Portuguese community of Macau often endowed them with funds for the building of these sanctuaries which in time became essentially Portuguese.

The earliest of the four Spanish foundations was São Francisco which was established by the Sevillian Pedro de Alfaro and by Juan Bautista just three years before the union of the two Crowns. A poor structure at the time of its foundation, São Francisco would later, in spite of stoic architectural lines, acquire a breathtaking beauty which still survived (no doubt after periodic renovation work) when the artist George Chinnery painted it some two hundred years later. Even in Chinnery's time its Romantic aspect was due to the location: Monastery and Church were set on a secluded promontory washed by the sea at the northernmost point of the Praia Grande and were thus situated outside the early settlement. There was at that time a natural fountain. It was the general effect of Monastery, heights, sea and fountain that a Spanish Franciscan had in mind in the late seventeenth century, when he wrote that although the Monastery was 'in the manner of our poor convents in Spain' it was, nonetheless, 'very happy'.

Behind a sober façade the interior of the Church was decorated with a set of large oil paintings depicting the life of St. Francis. Some of these, fortunately, survive, but in a pitiful state. Many of the works in the Church and Monastery were dispersed when the place was transformed into a military barracks between 1861 and 1866. Today the site of the Fort which was the first to repulse the Dutch siege of 1622 and which formed part of the complex almost from the start, can still be seen. But reclamation has spoilt the once-renowned vista, and the peal of São Francisco's bell, once muted only by the roaring wind and as much a part of Macau as was the gong of the A-Ma Temple, is silent.

*São Francisco Church*, detail
Ink drawing
George Chinnery, *c.* 1830
Crown Copyright Victoria and Albert Museum

*Santa Casa da Misericordia Church and tower*, detail
Ink drawing
George Chinnery, *c.* 1830
Crown Copyright Victoria and Albert Museum

Façade of São Paolo, detail of the Virgin and angels
*c.* 1635

Façade of São Paolo, detail of a Portuguese carrack and a fountain
c. 1635

Façade of São Paolo, detail of a cedar tree and of the Virgin stamping on a chimera
c. 1635

*The A-Ma Temple*, detail
Watercolour
Marciano Baptista, c. 1840
Museu Luis de Camões

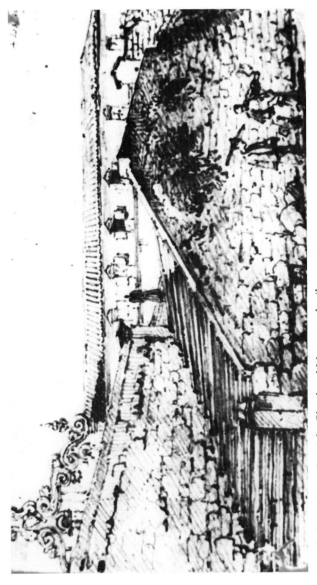

*Steps leading to Santo Agostinho Church and Monastery*, detail
Ink drawing
George Chinnery, *c.* 1830
Geographical Society, Lisbon

Macau at the turn of the century: looking north from the present-day
Governor's Praia Grande Palace
Charles Blackburn Collection

Macau at the turn of the century before the reclamation works: a view of
the north end of the Praia Grande looking towards São Francisco Fort
Charles Blackburn Collection

Museu Luis de Camões (formerly the Casa Garden), showing the upper storey and balustrade on the roof of the portico which have since been demolished
Photogravure
From a photograph by Albano de Magalhães, c. 1880
Museu Luis de Camões

The second of the Spanish monasteries, Santo Agostinho, was transferred to Portuguese monks by Philip II of Spain. Some three years after its original foundation it was built on the site now occupied by the Church of Our Lady of Grace, popularly known as Santo Agostinho. The Monastery has today disappeared and the present Church, built in a style that could be loosely described as Iberian neo-classical, is very likely the result of the reconstruction of 1875. At the beginning of the last century, however, its layout and style were quite different. A stepped alley rising above the Calçada de Santo Agostinho (formerly the Travessa das Onze Horas), gave access from the Praia to the Monastery and Church. The latter was graced by a late baroque or rococo façade which must have been unique in the Far East.

The Confraternity of Bom Jesus dos Passos was founded early in the history of Santo Agostinho and soon became an integral element in the life of the community. Today the Confraternity holds a famous procession early in Lent which derives from similar ceremonies dating back to the seventeenth century. The main image of the procession belongs to the type known in Hispanic baroque statuary as a Nazarene (a dramatic figure of Christ carrying the cross), and is worshipped throughout the year at the main altar of the Church. It is Macau's most revered Christian image, and is venerated as highly as A-Ma, the infant St. John the Baptist, and Kun-Yam. It leaves the main altar only at the time of the procession.

This Lent procession, which is a re-enactment of the Via Crucis in Jerusalem, Macau holds in common with other Christian communities in the region. In Goa and Manila there are quite similar ceremonies during this season. However, certain features are unique to Macau. The Bom Jesus leaves the Santo Agostinho Church of Our Lady of Grace borne on the shoulders of the members of the Confraternity. It is accompanied on its way by a Roman guard, the Blessed Sacrament, a chanting girl dressed as the Veronica of the Gospels, a military band and church and civic dignitaries. Crowds gather piously along the old streets of the city where by tradition the image must pass or linger, and believers and unbelievers unknowingly participate in Macau's Passion Play as the blood-stained image of the Nazarene is carried by. When the celebrants file into the Church to return the icon to its usual place for another year they are confronted by the sight of a statuary tableau of the Crucifixion which now rests on the main altar, lit by hundreds of candles. The Way of the Cross and this moving finale together represent Macau's most characteristic cultural manifestation.

There are other religious ceremonies which could be regarded as more truly Macanese, such as the feast of St. John the Baptist which is celebrated on 24 June. The infant St. John became patron of the city after the defeat of the Dutch in 1622. There is also the feast of Our Lady of Carmel, held on Taipa Island in July in one of the most charming Christian churches in the Far East. It could be argued that it is the A-Ma legends and the May rituals in A-Ma's honour in her Macau temple which are genuinely indigenous manifestations: in these forms the simple fisherfolk of the region give expression to their collective intuition of divine intervention in the affairs of men. In truth, both the Bom Jesus and A-Ma are local examples of cultural patterns with roots in Portugal and China. Together with Christmas and New Year, the former establishes an affiliation with Europe and with Portugal, while the latter and other Chinese rituals and celebrations, such as Chinese New Year, Qing Ming or the August Hungry Ghosts festival, are woven into the cultural fabric which unifies Chinese civilization.

The Chinese temples of Macau became places of pilgrimage from early on quite as much as its Christian churches.

Unfortunately, the dating of these buildings presents as many problems, if not more, as does the dating of the churches. One of the first to be recorded is the Kun-Yam Temple which is mentioned in sources dating from the Yuan dynasty (1279–1368). The Lin-Fong or Lotus Temple was founded at the end of the sixteenth century. Located on the southern tip of the dusty isthmus which gives access to Macau, it was temple and inn combined and provided a peaceful respite to the weary traveller on his arrival from China. The A-Ma Temple is recorded as having been built during the reign of Wan-Li of the Ming dynasty but since the Portuguese first arrived in the district at a village or bay called Haven of Ma, it is probable that at least a shrine existed before that. The fact that the three main Chinese temples of Macau are Buddhist is historically significant. The Ming Emperor Wan-Li had become a patron of Buddhism as a reaction against the previous emperor's Daoism and there was a renaissance of Buddhist architecture in China at this time.

The A-Ma Temple, more than any other temple in Macau, was intended to harmonize perfectly with nature in the classical Chinese manner. Its layout made use of a rugged hillock in a way that is unique in Macau. The pilgrim's spirit was uplifted as he climbed the rocky paths on which the four main pavilions are built, the jade-coloured tiles of the roofs emerging amidst the yellow and green bamboo groves or the venerable old trees whose colours changed with the seasons. The whole was set off by the flowing muddy waters of the river delta below. Originally, these waters came quite close to the Temple's embankment, as Captain Cook's draughtsman, John Webber, recorded at the end of the eighteenth century. Although the structures of the Temple site originate from the late Ming dynasty, they probably did not attain their present layout until the beginning of the eighteenth century. However, there were important later modifications, the most significant of which were made by the association of Fujian and Taicho merchants in 1828, and for which they paid 10,000 silver taels. It is this renovated temple which appears ten years later in the prints of the French painter, Auguste Borget, and in the drawings of George Chinnery.

Today, reclamation has transformed the site, and a polluted stream of cars and buses has replaced Webber's view. The desolate condition of the pavilions themselves is a world away from their former glory, but at least they have been spared the fate of São Paolo or São Francisco. The remote image of A-Ma (or Tin-Hau to the Cantonese), clad in the scarlet robes of an imperial bride, her face hidden, presides over all events in the soot-covered interior of the second pavilion of the first terrace.

The late baroque and rococo tastes of the Macanese, which prevailed in the city until superseded in the nineteenth century by the predilections of British East India merchants, were best exemplified by the Jesuit Church and Seminary of São José. The site that was chosen incorporated ground bought from the Augustinian order and an important plot of land known as the Mato Mofino which was donated to the Jesuits by the Senate. The foundations were laid in 1730 and the Church was finally inaugurated in 1758. Later drawings suggest that the undulations of the present façade, which are reminiscent of some Italian late baroque work, largely reproduce the original design. However this conjecture will only be confirmed if original elevations and plans of this building come to light. Certainly the twin towers of the front, topped by odd-looking domed vaults, and the large central dome were innovations. The latter was a daring novelty in Macau, which up to then had been a city of squat square towers and geometric lines. It may even be considered something of a rarity in China where, except in the construction of Islamic mosques, such domes were practically unknown. The experiment was never to be repeated in Macau; in neighbouring Hong Kong, the dome on a drum of the Law Courts was to become a prominent landmark when it appeared over one hundred years later.

# 9

# Gardens and Villas

As a result of the edicts of Emperor Qian-Long forbidding Europeans to reside in Guangzhou outside the trading season, from the middle of the eighteenth century foreigners began to rent and then purchase houses in Macau. The wealthiest of these newcomers were the supercargoes of the British East India Company: in the 1780s one of their number named William Fitzhugh rented the Casa Garden, a country villa just outside the city walls. Like the Church of São José it had originally belonged to the Jesuits: after their expulsion it passed into the hands of an administrator appointed by Goa.

The grounds of the property incorporated the Rocks of Camões, Macau's monument to the great poet Luis de Camões, and the whole site had previously been known by this name. It seems very probable that Fitzhugh was responsible for the renovation of the property, transforming the woods into an extensive garden in the English manner. The residence, which included the building today housing the Luis de Camões Museum, became known to the foreign community as the Casa Garden.

During his tenancy Fitzhugh welcomed many visitors to his garden, now one of the largest and most beautiful in a city where private compounds tended to be small. One of his guests was the French scientist, La Pérouse, who studied the earth's magnetism there. After Fitzhugh's departure, the property was let to another East India merchant, James Drummond: during Drummond's tenancy, the botanist David Stromach studied the plants in the garden. Stromach was a member of the historic embassy of Lord Macartney, and it seems very probable that

Macartney himself wandered along the wooded paths of the garden during his stay at the villa in 1794 on return from Beijing.

Two years after Macartney's visit the Casa Garden passed into the hands of the Leal Senado. Manuel Pereira appears to have been the next owner: he bought it from the Senado in 1815 after he had become a Senator. It seems that it was during Pereira's ownership that the gardens began to deteriorate.

Mystery still surrounds almost every aspect of the history of the Casa Garden: we do not know the names of the first owner and the architect nor do we have much idea of the original appearance of the house. But one may surmise that, since local mansions of the early nineteenth century consisted of large, roomy, two-storeyed structures composed of *piano nobile* and basement, this would also have been true of the Casa Garden. It is, in fact, the same elevation that exists today, although the interior decoration of the building, and possible modifications to the ground-plan at the back attest to several quite radical transformations since the late nineteenth century. During the latter period, even the front elevation was modified, as illustrations of the time show. A shallow rectangular storey, some 40 feet wide and 20 feet deep, was added to the main entrance portico. This portico is made of granite and stands at the top of a grand flight of granite steps. It has two unusual square Doric pillars which support a small masonry balcony. When the shallow storey was pulled down early in our century, a classical balustrade (now missing) with ornamental urns was added to the roof of the building, matching the balustrade of the nearby garden walls. Some of the latter and the exquisite work and effect of the ornamental urns still survive but they are fast disappearing due to typhoons and other vicissitudes. The existing neo-classical decoration in the interior of the building also gives some idea of what it looked like in the eighteenth century.

From the 1770s the British East India Company had started renting houses along the Praia Grande until eventually it occupied four. Together with the Governor's Palace and certain other private houses belonging to wealthy Portuguese or foreigners, these were built in the neo-classical architecture which would remain fashionable in Macau until well into the following century. The great majority of these houses were built with brick, rubble and wood, and faced with stucco, a form of construction typical of Macanese architecture. At a later date, when the technique had degenerated, not only the details of interiors, but often also the outside classical orders or pilasters, were simply moulded in stucco in true wedding-cake manner.

At the beginning of the nineteenth century, however, the style had great charm and was much appreciated by Harriet Low, an American whose uncle was director of Russell and Company. The glass-roofed attic of her uncle's house next to the Cathedral commanded a splendid view of the Praia Grande. Writing between 1829 and 1833, Harriet tells of her vivid impressions of the brilliant whites of the houses of the Praia Grande and of the villa at the Casa Garden. With the Romantic enthusiasm of the age she praises the grandeur of the Church and Fort of São Francisco. Harriet Low was to be one of the first two American women to set foot in China and is the subject of a fine portrait by the artist George Chinnery.

Macau now offered its hospitality to a number of interesting Europeans, from various walks of life, who were greatly to enrich the city's art and culture. The painter George Chinnery spent a great part of his working life in the city, where he finally died. Another artist, Auguste Borget, passed only half a year in the territory between 1838 and 1839, but many of his best works belong to his sojourn in Macau. In these years the city also sheltered the Swedish scholar, Andrew Ljungstedt, the first historian of Macau, and the great Anglican missionary, Robert

Morrison, both of whom, like Chinnery, are buried near the Casa Garden. These men were representatives of the renaissance of Western humanism which transcended Europe's geographical frontiers.

In the quaint world of the sketches and paintings of George Chinnery, the picturesque image of Macau is the subject for a type of cityscape such as had been popularized in England by Italian painters. Today we can still trace the painter's artistic itinerary: from his home behind São Lourenço Church, he turns down São Lourenço Street, then heads for Santo Agostinho or the British East India mansions along the Praia Grande, and finally explores the Senate and São Domingos Square. Together with the A-Ma Temple and other stops along the Porto Interior, these all became favourite haunts of professional or amateur painters visiting Macau. Moreover, the view from the Praia Grande of gilded dawns and dusks and hazy silhouettes of mountainous islands beyond, to which residents of the fashionable compounds in the Praia were treated every day, would suit the most spiritual of Romantic tastes.

The most impressive construction of the second half of the nineteenth century was the Guia Lighthouse, built in 1865 to a height of 13.5 metres on the summit of Guia Hill which is itself over 80 metres high. It was erected to the design of the Macanese Carlos Vicente da Rocha, with funds donated by the firm of H.D. Margesson. The first lighthouse on the China coast, it was symbolic of the confidence regained by the colony under Governor Coelho do Amaral, to whom the Praia Grande urbanization, including the planting of its famous trees, was due. Amaral was also responsible for the erection of São Francisco Fort and the military barracks on the site of the old Monastery. Then as now these military establishments were an embellishment to the city, albeit their siting was controversial.

The year 1874 saw the construction of two large public

buildings: the Viscount de São Januário Hospital which was designed along neo-Gothic lines, and the Moorish Barracks which employed a neo-Moorish style. This variety of architectural styles was a reflection of a contemporary eclecticism of taste in Europe. Many private citizens in Macau responded enthusiastically to this trend and had their homes adorned with a diversity of exquisite façades that were often unashamedly whimsical. Unfortunately the 1874 typhoon was to interfere with many of these developments, causing damage to the Moorish Barracks only months after its opening, uprooting Amaral's Praia Grande trees, toppling the highest domes of the towers of the Cathedral (which had been rebuilt in 1850), and even partly destroying the proud Lighthouse at Guia.

Even before this typhoon, the modern decline of Macau had begun. However this did not prevent the erection of several of the city's most attractive buildings in this period. During King Pedro V's reign a theatre bearing his name was built to the plans of the Macanese Pedro Marques in 1858. Its present façade took shape in 1873 and later following designs by the Barão do Cercal. Equally attractive is São Lourenço Church, whose present appearance must be largely the result of the 1897–8 reconstructions, with designs by the architect Augusto César d'Abreu Nunes. Both of these well-known buildings are characteristic of Macau's late neo-classical style, but it can be seen from Chinnery's sketches of São Lourenço that the large single nave and twin east towers were features of an earlier building. The rebuilding or renovation of São Lourenço, with applied Doric decoration outside, and colossal Corinthian pilasters in the interior, make this one of the finest examples of neo-classical architecture anywhere.

However, the grandest example of this late neo-classical phase in Macau was not the house of a Portuguese, nor of any other European. It was to be found in the private mansion and grounds of Lou Kau (Lou Cheok-chi). Amidst the famous Chinese gardens designed by Lei Tai-chun and Lau Kat-lok, there stands a pavilion supported by the most graceful of Corinthian columns. The Lous were a family of high rank from Guangzhou, and counted scholars and artists amongst their members. Construction of pavilions and other structures went on into the next century, when Lou Kau's eldest son, Lou Lim-yeok, who became a merchant and diplomat of great standing in Macau (and was awarded the Order of Christ in 1925 by the Portuguese Government), inherited the property. After it passed out of the hands of Lou Lim-yeok's heirs to be used as a Chinese school, the compound met a fate similar to that of the Casa Garden, Macau's other great private garden of a hundred years earlier. It was rescued from a slow decay by the wife of a recent governor of Macau who offered it to the community as a public garden.

During the urbanization of the late nineteenth and early twentieth centuries, the neo-classical style was also applied to the apartment blocks built in São Lázaro, the old quarter which had been developed in 1809 as an area for Chinese converts or 'new Christians' under the initiative of the Spanish friar, José Segui. This had also been the site of Dom Melchior Carneiro's leprosarium. In the São Lázaro and Largo do Senado houses and elsewhere, as well as in the Leal Senado building which itself was rebuilt at the end of the nineteenth century, classical orders were either abolished, leaving only large pediments, or were reduced to applied pilasters sometimes framing arcaded balconies. At this time there were also constructed a number of private villas of distinction, one of the most pleasant of which was the summer residence of Sir Robert Ho-Tung. This villa, with its airy arcades, was donated by this philanthropist to the Portuguese Government.

There are, however, sorry indications that the insensitive

restoration and repainting of historic buildings that is evident today was already commonplace in the late nineteenth century. The disturbing callousness shown towards their heritage by the Macanese has been as harmful as typhoons or the misunderstandings of unsympathetic foreigners. One of the most vocal critics of this well-meant vandalism was the Portuguese expatriate and champion of the Macanese, Manuel da Silva Mendes, who was painfully aware of the harm being done. But even he was blind to the merits of some of Macau's most characteristic buildings. In 1919 he wrote that there was nothing in Macau's religious architecture which deserved one's attention. Whilst he admitted that São Domingos had agreeable lines, he could not help but exclaim 'look at its execution; look at the materials: granite bases, shafts and capitals of brick and mortar ... One feels like having the whole thing pulled down. And worst of all, it is washed in blue with the doors smeared green'. We would certainly have shared his horror of the blue décor, so different to today's yellow wash, and he is perfectly accurate about the materials used. But Silva Mendes does not appreciate Macau's achievement in evolving a highly original local variant of Portuguese architecture in the face of the persistent obstruction of Chinese building regulations (which were directed against the erection of durable structures and laid down rules about building materials).

Silva Mendes went on to report that in the ten years from about 1905 to 1915 the Public Works Department had spent several hundred thousand patacas on plans to embellish the city and that, in certain respects, the aspect of Macau had indeed improved. But he also complained that 'a stroll through the city streets reveals a complete absence of artistic feeling, both in private works and in those of the state. Previously there were a good number of buildings, especially in Chinese style, of which one could note, if not refinements of art, at least indications of good taste ... Everything, or almost everything, has been pulled down.' When he writes of improvements in the city's appearance, Silva Mendes must have had in mind the São Lázaro urbanization as well as certain works of engineering. But reclamation along the Praia Grande had robbed the city of part of the celebrated walk on the north side of the strand, and most of the many beautiful and historic buildings were disappearing.

Sadly our century has also seen the demise of some of Macau's most cherished traditions. The *do*, which had become the traditional costume for women, has vanished. If there was ever anything which could be called local folk music, it is nowhere to be heard today. Certain festive ornaments and traditions of Cantonese origin such as the festive *pai-lou* and ceremonial dragon boats so prominent in the history of the city have largely disappeared.

The *lingua de Macau*, Macau's own way of speaking Portuguese, in which the Portuguese language has undergone one of its most sprightly and gentle mutations, has only just survived. What does remain, which could be called Macanese, reflects an ingenious mixture of Portuguese and Cantonese traditions relating to all stages of family life such as weddings, births and funerals. Macau would not be Macau without its lion dances, the constant explosion of red firecrackers (to ward off evil spirits), its Portuguese wines and Latin melodies.

In the early twentieth century, the desire for modernization led to the promotion of some daring engineering schemes, but only a few of these were to be carried out. Some of the reasons for this have been given a brief outline in Chapter Seven of this book. Certain of these projects, involving land reclamation, are still under consideration today. They would have transformed the face of the Macau peninsula and would have swept away the surviving section of the Praia Grande, the northern section of which is already enclosed within reclaimed land. The schemes of the 1920s were mercifully never put into effect.

The past, in Macau more poignantly so than elsewhere, has come and gone. Reclamation of land has introduced the rigidity of geometry to the peninsula's natural configuration. The new Lisboa Hotel and Casino and the jetfoil and hydrofoil terminuses for Hong Kong have been amongst the most conspicuous additions to the city. Even more impressive is the one-mile-long Taipa bridge built in 1974 by the Portuguese engineer, Edgar Cardoso, which has radically changed the spatial orientation of the city and effectively expanded its limits out towards the islands of Taipa and Coloane.

Who would have thought, on looking today from the north Praia Grande parapet across the vastness of the oceans, that it was over that horizon that the first tiny caravels from Portugal arrived over four hundred years ago with their frail, impudent cargo of human hopes and ambitions.

# Selected Bibliography

All translations in the text from the Portuguese and French are by the author. Most of the originals are to be found in this bibliography.

Boxer, C.R., *Fidalgos in the Far East, 1550–1770* (The Hague, Martinus Nijhoff, 1948; reprinted Hong Kong, Oxford University Press, 1968).

——*Macau Three Hundred Years Ago* (Macau, Imprensa Nacional, 1942; reprinted Hong Kong, Heinemann (Asia), 1984, under the title *Seventeenth Century Macau*).

——*The Christian Century in Japan, 1549–1650* (Berkeley, University of California Press, 1967).

——*The Great Ship from Amacon* (Lisbon, 1959).

Braga, J.M., 'China Landfall, 1513: Jorge Álvares' Voyage to China' *Boletim do Instituto Português de Hong Kong*, No. 4, June 1955.

——*Primeiro Acordo Luso–Chines* (Macau, 1939).

——*The Western Pioneers and Their Discovery of Macau* (Macau, Imprensa Nacional, 1949).

Camoens, Luis Vaz de, *The Lusiads*, translated by W.C. Atkinson (Harmondsworth, Penguin, 1952).

Chan, Albert, *The Glory and Fall of the Ming Dynasty* (Norman, University of Oklahoma Press, 1982).

Coates, Austin, *Prelude to Hong Kong* (London, Routledge and Kegan Paul, 1966).

Elliott, J.H., *Imperial Spain 1469–1716* (Harmondsworth, Pelican Books, 1976).

Gomes, A.L., *Esboço da Historia de Macau, 1511–1849* (Macau, Repartição Provincial dos Serviços de Economia e Estatistica Geral, 1957).

Gomes, L.G., *Efemeridas da Historia de Macau* (Macau, 1954).

——(trans.), *Monografia de Macau par Tcheong-ü-lâm e Ian-Kuong-iâm* (Macau, Imprensa Nacional, 1950).

Lessa, A., *A Historia e os Homens da Primeira Republica Democratica do Oriente* (Macau, Imprensa Nacional, 1974).

Ljungstedt, Andrew, *An Historical Sketch of the Portuguese Settlements in China* (Boston, James Munroe, 1836).

Montalto de Jesus, C.A., *Historic Macao: International Traits in China Old and New* (Hong Kong, Kelly and Walsh, 1902; second edition, Macau, Salesian Printing Press, 1926, reprinted Hong Kong, Oxford University Press, 1984).

Pires, Benjamim Videira, *A Viagem de Comércio Macau–Manila Nos Séculos XVI a XIX* (Macau, Imprensa Nacional, 1971).

——*Embaixada Martir* (Macau, Centro Informação e Turismo, 1965).

——*O IV Centenário dos Jesuítas em Macau (1564–1964)* (Macau, 1964).

Ptak, Roderich, *Portugal in China, Kurzer Abriss Der Portugiesich–Chinesischen Beziehungen und Der Geschichte Macaus* (Klemmerberg Verlag, 1980).

Schumann, Franz, and Schell, Orville (ed.), *Imperial China (China Readings): The Eighteenth and Nineteenth Centuries* (Harmondsworth, Penguin, 1977).

Serrão, Joaquim Verissimo, *Historia de Portugal*, vols. 3 and 4 (Verbo, 1980).

Silva Mendes, Manuel da, *Colectanea de Artigos de Manuel da Silva Mendes*, vol. 1 (Macau, 1963).

Teixeira, Manuel, *A Gruta de Camoes em Macau* (Macau, Imprensa Nacional, 1977).

——*Os Militares em Macau* (Macau, Comando Territorial

Independente Imprensa Nacional, 1975).

—— *Templo Chines da Barra Ma-Kok-Miu* (Macau, Tipografia da Missao, 1979).

—— *Toponîmia de Macau* (Macau, Imprensa Nacional, 1979).

—— *Macau No Seculo XVIII* (Macau, Imprensa Nacional, 1984).

Usellis, W.R., *The Origin of Macao* (unpublished dissertation, University of Chicago, 1958).

# Index

# INDEX

# INDEX

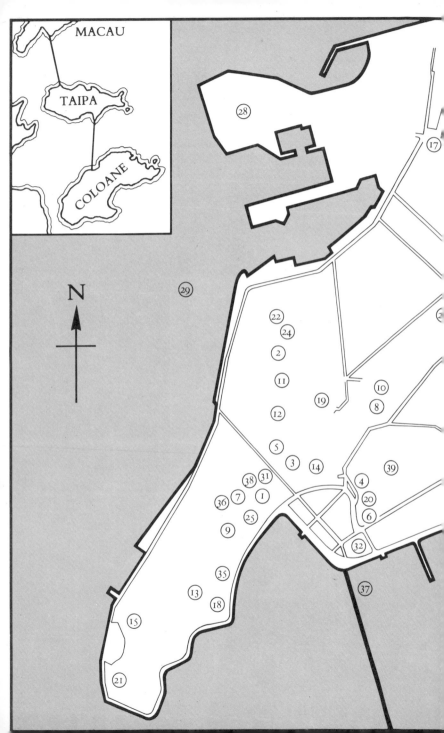